Apocalyptic Realism

Russian and East European Studies in Aesthetics and the Philosophy of Culture

Willis H. Truitt
General Editor

Vol. 1

PETER LANG
New York • Washington, D.C./Baltimore • San Francisco
Bern • Frankfurt am Main • Berlin • Vienna • Paris

Yvonne Howell

Apocalyptic Realism

The Science Fiction
of Arkady and Boris Strugatsky

PETER LANG
New York • Washington, D.C./Baltimore • San Francisco
Bern • Frankfurt am Main • Berlin • Vienna • Paris

Library of Congress Cataloging-in-Publication Data

Howell, Yvonne.
   Apocalyptic realism: the science fiction of Arkady and Boris
Strugatsky / Yvonne Howell.
     p.   cm. — (Russian and East European studies in aesthetics and
the philosophy of culture; v. 1)
   Includes bibliographical references and index.
   1. Strugatskiĭ, Arkadiĭ Natanovich—Criticism and interpretation.
2. Strugatskiĭ, Boris Natanovich—Criticism and interpretation. 3. Science
fiction, Russian—History and criticism. I. Title. II. Series.
PG3476.S78835Z69   1994   891.73'44—dc20   92-37988
ISBN 0-8204-1962-1   CIP
ISSN 1065-9374

Die Deutsche Bibliothek-CIP-Einheitsaufnahme

Howell, Yvonne:
Apocalyptic realism: the science fiction of Arkady and Boris Strugatsky /
Yvonne Howell. - New York; Bern; Berlin; Frankfurt/M.; Paris; Wien: Lang,
1994
   (Russian and East European studies in aesthetics and the philosophy of
culture; Vol. 1)
   ISBN 0-8204-1962-1
NE: GT

Cover design by James F. Brisson.

The paper in this book meets the guidelines for permanence and durability of
the Committee on Production Guidelines for Book Longevity of the
Council on Library Resources.

© Peter Lang Publishing, Inc., New York 1994

Printed in the United States of America.

Contents

Preface and Acknowledgements

In 1967, a nationally distributed poll found that four of the Strugatskys' novels ranked first, second, sixth, and tenth place, as the most popular works of science fiction in the Soviet Union. The Strugatskys' *Hard to Be a God* (1964) and *Monday Begins on Saturday* (1965) ranked in first and second place, resp., above Russian translations of Bradbury's *Martian Chronicles*, Stanislaw Lem's *Solaris*, and Asimov's *I, Robot*. For the next two decades, the Strugatskys' popularity among Soviet readers was regarded as almost a law of nature, separate from and beyond the statistics which shuffled the relative popularity rankings of all other science fiction writers. Obviously, readership polls do not rank literary merit, nor the power of the work to retain its significance for successive generations. Nevertheless, the Strugatskys' consistent success over three decades of immanent change in the science fiction genre, as well as ideological change in Soviet literary policies, leads to the question: How did a professional translator and war-time interpreter of Japanese (Arkady Natanovich Strugatsky, 1925-1991) and his brother, an astrophysicist formerly employed at the Pulkovo Observatory (Boris Natanovich Strugatsky, b. 1933) strike such a chord among the educated Russian reading public by writing science fiction?

The Strugatskys began writing science fiction together in the late 1950s. They immediately became the most popular writers in their genre—but unlike popular science fiction writers in the West, their fame soon extended well outside of any science fiction ghetto, and even outside the realm of popular or mass literature. With each new novel, it became increasingly evident that the Strugatskys were mainly writing for, and read by, the so-called intelligentsia. The intelligentsia has been defined by a least one wit in the succinct but emphatic formulation "people who *think*." In other words, the intelligentsia does not wholly coincide with the country's academic and professional elites, many of whom reached their positions only by thinking what was officially correct. It includes individuals from all walks of life who have cultivated their intellectual and ethical concerns. Not surprisingly, though, the Strugatskys' most devoted fans were those involved in the sciences and technological fields.

The body of critical literature on the Strugatskys' works is disproportionately small, compared to the enormous popularity of their works in the Soviet Union. One reason for the relative paucity of critical attention accorded the Strugatskys before glasnost is mainly political. During the post-Khrushchev years, the Strugatskys maintained a precarious and somewhat anomalous position as writers neither wholly approved of, nor yet officially black-listed. Increasingly hostile official criticism of their work in the late sixties was enough to make them circumspect to the point of near silence throughout the seventies. In other words, their enemies soon had almost nothing left to criticize, while their friends and supporters had either emigrated, or proved their friendship and support by remaining conspiratorially silent, rather than exacerbate the Strugatskys' troubles by providing insightful criticism of avowedly anti-Marxist works. Western critics, by and large, reacted in the same way, in reverse: if the authors were not dissidents, they were probably not worth criticizing. Moreover, they belonged to neither of the most visible mainstream prose movements in Russian literature of the seventies—the urban prose movement exemplified by the works of Iurii Trifonov, and the village prose movement championed by Valentin Rasputin and many others. Thus, the present study covers much ground in redressing the imbalance between the significance of the Strugatskys' work in contemporary Russian culture and the lack of scholarly attention it has heretofore received. It does not, however, offer a general interpretation of the Strugatskys' place within the broader area of international science fiction. Rather, this study provides a view of the Strugatskys' place within the context of their own literary and cultural milieu.

This study was conceived before the advent of Gorbachev's glasnost policy changed the way books are censored, published (or not published), and read in the former Soviet Union. The policy of "openness," which had gained considerable momentum in the last years of Arkady Strugatsky's life, had no direct effect on the quality of the Strugatskys' writing. Now that all of the Strugatskys' novels are being edited and published in their original, uncensored versions, it has become clear that the Strugatskys, like many of their more illustrious predecessors, can be counted among those writers whose non-canonical works are being rediscovered after years of suppression. The postscript to this study on "apocalyptic realism" suggests that in post-glasnost Russia, the Strugatskys' works will be read and enjoyed as much for their historical value as models of a unique scientific culture (the isolated, yet brilliant communities which made the Soviet scientific endeavor successful), as for their fictional qualities.

More people contributed to this study, as often as not in the course of casual but invaluable conversations, than I can acknowledge here by name. I would like to express my warm appreciation to all my colleagues at Dartmouth College for their support. I am especially grateful to Lev Loseff, John Kopper, Kevin Reinhart, and Carol Bardenstein for their expertise and help with early chapter drafts and unfamiliar materials. I would like to thank Eric Rabkin for his attentive reading and advice in the early stages of this project; Ken Knoespel for his encouragement in later stages; and Daniil Alexandrov for his valuable insights. I am grateful to the University of Richmond for supporting the completion of the book.

In Russia, I owe much to Tanya Lobasheva, whose friendship and unique heritage have always been a source of great inspiration. I am most grateful for the unpublished material and overwhelming hospitality supplied by the exuberant "Ludens" in Moscow, St. Petersburg, and Abakan; and to Elena Romanovna Gaginskaia, who introduced me to Boris Strugatsky. This book is dedicated to Arkady Strugatsky, who died in October, 1991.

I have assumed that many readers will not be speakers of Russian. I have even assumed that the tendency to quote more, rather than less, out of the Strugatskys' latest works will benefit those readers who want a taste of otherwise untranslated and inaccessible material. For ease of reading, in the main text I use a modified Library of Congress system of transliteration and maintain the anglicized spelling of familiar names and titles. In the notes and bibliography, I adhere more strictly to the Library of Congress system, but without diacritical marks.

Introduction

The epigraph to the last published piece of fiction Arkady and Boris Strugatsky wrote together is a quote from the Japanese writer Ryunosuke Akutagawa:

To call a despot a despot
has always been dangerous.
But in our times
To call a slave a slave
is equally dangerous.

A cast of characters follows. The work is a play, and the cast consists of a middle-aged professor and his wife, their two grown sons, and a few of their friends and neighbors. There is also "A Figure in Black." Otherwise, there is no hint of anything out of the ordinary in the opening scene:

A room doubling as living room and office in the apartment of Professor Kirsanov. Center back—two large windows with closed shutters. Between them stands an antique desk-bureau with numerous drawers. On top of the desk is an open typewriter, stacks of paper, folders, several large dictionaries, a mess.
   In the middle of the room, center stage—an oval table covered with a tablecloth, electric samovar, tea cups, sugar bowl, a bowl filled with cookies. On the left, with its side to the audience, stands a large color television. Having tea while watching the Soviet Congress of Deputies in session are . . . :

KIRSANOV: That jerk butt in again! I can't stand him . . .
BAZARIN: Could be worse. Zoya Sergeevna, just a drop more tea, if you would . . .
ZOYA SERGEEVNA: *(pouring tea)* Do you want it strong?
BAZARIN: No, no, not too strong, it s already nighttime . . .
KIRSANOV: *(with disgust)* I mean *really*, what an obnoxious mug! In Portugal or somewhere, on the basis of that ugly mug alone the guy would never get elected into Parliament! (92-93)[1]

Presently a mysterious figure in black appears in the doorway. Although he explains his unwelcome penetration into the apartment—"your bell doesn't work and the door was half-open"— it is clear that he can and will get into any apartment he needs to, at any time of night. After perusing Kirsanov's passport, he hands him an official-looking paper, asks him to sign a receipt, and disappears. The document is addressed to "Rich People of the City of Peter! All rich people in the city of Peter and its environs must appear today, the twelfth of January, by eight a.m., on the square in front of . . ." The place, what to bring, and what to leave behind are designated. In a few minutes Pinsky, the Kirsanov's upstairs neighbor and dear family friend, shows up in his robe and slippers with a similar document in hand, this one addressed to "Yids of the City of Peter! . . ." The derogatory address to the Jews erases any ambiguity about the nature of the summons, and both the "rich" Kirsanov and the Jew Pinsky fight back a growing sense of helplessness.

Thus begins the Strugatskys' play *Yids of the City of Peter, or Gloomy Discussions by Candlelight,* written and published in 1990. During the 1991 spring season, it was being performed on a regular basis in the theaters of Leningrad, the city known to its inhabitants as St. Petersburg, Peter's city, or, simply, *"Piter."* At first glance the play seems to be something new and anomalous to the rest of the Strugatskys' work. Did the authors get carried away by the imperative of glasnost, and abandon literature of the fantastic for barely disguised journalism?

On the contrary, for all its topical, surface realism, the play is entirely typical of the Strugatskys' brand of fantastic literature. The play's fast-paced, suspenseful plot is based on conventions of "cheap" detective and science fiction literature, but it is grounded in the realm of serious literature by weighty philosophical diatribes delivered by the main characters. At their best, as in *City of Peter,* the Strugatskys integrate the light and the weighty, the mundane and the metaphysical, without reconciling the ambiguity between different poles. All of the characteristic features of the Strugatskys' mature writing are present in this play. The epigraph is chosen from Arkady Strugatsky's favorite Japanese author, and, more importantly, it succinctly conveys the Strugatskys' most consistent sociopolitical theme. Character and dialog (whether or not they ostensibly belong to a future and/or alien time and place) mimic the norm for contemporary Soviet urban intellectuals with such felicity, that one is often correct in assuming that a real-life prototype exists among the authors' acquaintances. Furthermore, the specific details of the setting belong unmistakably to the authors' contemporary milieu. "Zero-transport cabins" and other superficial sci-fi gadgetry in the early novels notwithstanding, the Strugatskys' material world almost always reflects contemporary Soviet standards, e.g., the professor has a manual typewriter in a portable case, not a computer. Likewise, every Russian reader can picture the bowl and the tasteless store-bought cookies in it: both are churned out in uniform size and color by a centrally-planned economy. Yet it is precisely this drab reality that generates a second, metaphysical reality: beyond his probable identity as a KGB agent, the figure in black also has the aura of Mozart's Black Visitor from Pushkin's drama *Mozart and Salieri*.

One of the truisms of science fiction genre studies is that in science fiction, reality is "made strange" in light of a single fantastic premise. Darko Suvin defined science fiction as a genre which "takes off from a fictional ("literary") hypothesis and develops it with totalizing ("scientific") rigor."[2] The Strugatskys' work conforms to this definition, but with a twist. Their depiction of ordinary Soviet reality is indeed "made strange" by a single extraordinary premise. The play's fantastic premise, which casts a shadow of the supernatural over everyday scenes, is that in the year of 1990, at the height of Gorbachev's glasnost reforms, the country could suddenly revert to the dark ages of terror, pogroms, and totalitarianism. In this instance, though, the vector between life and literary hypothesis reversed its direction. On August 19, 1991, four months after the *City of Peter* was published, an unsuccessful coup by communist hardliners turned the Strugatskys' "fantastic" literary hypothesis into an averted political reality. For a Russian writer, it has perhaps always been more gratifying to see life *avert* art, rather than life imitate art. In the following study of the Strugatskys' work, I will try to establish the patterns of interplay between the Strugatskys' depictions of Soviet reality and the "fantastic premises" they have derived from the heritage of Russian literature and culture as a whole.

This book is not a systematic overview of the Strugatskys'
career or a general interpretation of the Strugatskys' place in
world science fiction. Rather, I approach the Strugatskys' work
from within the history and evolution of mainstream Russian
literature, and seek to define the Strugatskys' place in the context of already established, native Russian literary and cultural
traditions. One of the side benefits of this approach is that it
sheds some light on the nature of the Strugatskys' reception in
the West. It is striking that the Soviet Union's most popular
science fiction writers have not enjoyed the success of, for
instance, Poland's Stanislaw Lem in the Anglo-American market. The problem of (some) inadequate English translations
aside, the surprisingly modest success the Strugatskys' work has
encountered in the West may have to do in part with readers'
general lack of familiarity with the profoundly Russian questions addressed in the Strugatskys' use of an ostensibly international genre.

More importantly, I hope to fill a large gap in existing criticism (both Soviet and Western), which has tended to concentrate only on the allegorical possibilities of science fiction. It
has been tempting to ignore *how* the Strugatskys write, in order
to concentrate on their *message,* which is presumably more
earth-bound and politically current than their intergalactic settings might lead a disapproving censor to believe. To vindicate
this point, critics have often sought to extract and isolate a
social, political, or ethical stance out of the Strugatskys' work, as
if to prove that *this* science fiction is not simply escapist entertainment. The best pieces of this type of criticism have suc-
ceeded precisely in establishing the Strugatskys' reputation as
writers who are primarily concerned with serious philosophical,
social, and ethical questions.

On the other hand, the Strugatskys' enduring popularity is
assumed to be part and parcel of the genre they write
in—science fiction is an inherently "popular" genre, and the
Strugatskys "happen" to be extremely talented practitioners.
Science fiction, like the two other popular genre forms with
which it often intermingles—the detective or crime novel and
the adventure/historical novel—belongs to the realm of popular
literature insofar as it typically provides exotic characters

and/or settings and a suspenseful plot within the context of an established set of conventions. Familiar science fiction conventions include the confrontation between human and alien life forms, the conflict between human values and technological progress, the juxtaposition of past and future societies, and so forth. Any serious departure from the genre's familiar, formulaic underlying premises constitutes a perceived departure from the genre altogether, and usually entails confusion among readers.[3] In other words, it is taken for granted that the Strugatskys' science fiction is accessible and entertaining in a way that ponderous mainstream realism and sophisticated avant-garde experimentation is not. As such, however, it seems to hardly merit serious critical attention at all—the common, and often deserved fate of popular literary subgenres both in the East and in the West. A Russian critic speculated that the surprising lack of Strugatsky criticism, even after three decades of unabated popularity, is due precisely to the inherent lack of esteem accorded to the science fiction genre:

> What is at issue here? Perhaps the conviction that has formed among critics . . . that the fantastic [science fiction] is about something exotic and detached from real life, unrelated to the problems of contemporary life? Once this is so, then it does not deserve to be a topic of conversation among serious people. . . .[4]

Clearly, some of the critical confusion—resulting for the most part in silence—has been perpetuated by the unresolved incongruity between the Strugatskys as writers in a popular, "mass" genre and, on another level, as spokesmen for at least one whole generation of Soviet intellectuals. Mikhail Lemkhin inadvertently poses the question this study sets out to answer when he writes:

> I'm afraid that I cannot explain why, but it is certain that for me these three tales—*Hard to Be a God, Roadside Picnic,* and *One Billion Years Until the End of the World*—are not only landmarks in my life, but representative of whole chunks of my life which were lived under the constellation of these tales. And I know for certain that I am not the only such reader.
>
> The question of [their] popularity is a separate, special topic. Here I address a different topic: why and how the questions which concerned the Strugatskys were not only their own questions. The Strugatskys' evolution, their sense of where and how they exist in the world—follows

a path fairly typical for a large part of the intelligentsia, in particular
for the scientific intelligentsia. Without a doubt it is because of this fact
that the Strugatskys are among our most widely-read authors. . . . [5]

In order to define the nature of the relationship between the
Strugatskys' use of popular genre forms and their importance
as "serious writers" for the intelligentsia, I explore two
questions in this book:

• What techniques do the authors develop to encode an
open-ended philosophical discussion or sociopolitical debate
into the formulaic structures of science fiction, detective, and
adventure story literature?

• How are the conventional plots, characters, and settings of
the popular genres shaped into modern myths for the intelligentsia to live by,"under the constellation of these tales"?

The Early Publications

The Strugatskys made their debut with the 1958 short story
Izvne (From Without), followed by several science fiction and
space adventure novellas and short stories.[6] The novel *Hard to
Be a God* (1964) is the first decisive landmark in the development of the Strugatskys' work. All of the novels and short stories prior to 1964 can be considered to belong to their early
phase. In this phase, the answer to "the question which always
interested us . . . where are we going . . . after the XX Party
Congress?" seems to be already evident: the road to the
"radiant communist future," temporarily detoured by Stalinism,
once again lies ahead. The first short story, "From Without"
(1958), takes place in the abstract present; subsequently, temporal and spacial horizons expand into the future and onto other
planets and solar systems, until, by the mid-twenty-second century depicted in *Noon: 22nd Century* (1962) utopian communism
reigns on Earth. The hallmark of the Strugatskys' idyllic future
world is that it combines both poles of traditional Russian
utopian thought: the vision of pastoral happiness, in simple
harmony with nature, is implicit in the depiction of green
garden-cities, and in the child-like curiosity, rather than
Faustian pride, of the stories' scientist-heroes. On the other

hand, the utopian dream of artificially created abundance and the omnipotence of human technology is also realized in the Strugatskys' twenty-second century. Hardy hybrid cattle whose flesh is as white and delicate as crab meat, non-polluting, instantaneous methods of transportation, and the characters' fleeting worries over what to do with an excess of time and luxury are the specific traits of this vision.

Although the main dramatic conflict in the early novels and stories is "between the good and the better," the authors succeed in populating their future world with refreshingly quirky and humorous characters. Furthermore, even in the earliest utopian future history, setting and dialog retain the immediacy and mimetic power of contemporary realistic prose.[7] The novels and short stories of this phase of the Strugatskys' writing have little relevance to the main topics treated in this study. They are essentially one-dimensional, extrapolatory works of science fiction which reflect the general optimistic ethos of the "thaw" generation. Total harmony between social utopia and unabated scientific progress is threatened for the first time in *Far Rainbow* (1963), which is set sometime in the twenty-third century. A series of physics experiments conducted in the idyllic scientific research colony on the planet Rainbow creates a tidal wave of matter/energy which the scientists cannot control. Most of the planet is evacuated, but the scientists who must remain await death by the unstoppable black wave with quiet heroism and a clear conscience.

About half of the works written in the sixties belong to a loosely connected future history series. A few stock characters and futuristic gadgets (e.g., instantaneous transport boothes) reappear over and over again. The basic premise of the earliest future history cycle remains the same: some kind of international world communism (no longer necessarily idyllic) reigns on Earth, and the stars and planets in our galaxy, as well as those of the "Periphery" (beyond our galaxy) are being actively explored and/or colonized. Another key feature which unites all the future history novels is the concept of "progressorism." "Progressors" are missionaries from Earth, who, armed with humanity's twenty-first century wisdom and technology, attempt to help less developed societies on other planets. All of the

novels included in the loosely connected future history cycle
share the theme of progressorism, and most of them are structured as parables: the Progressor plot creates a model in which
the distance between more and less socially, politically, and ecologically advanced societies is simply projected into interplane-
tary space.

The 1964 novel *Hard to Be a God* marks a turning point in the
future history cycle, and in the Strugatskys' development as
novelists. To this day, *Hard to Be a God* ranks as one of the
most popular works of science fiction ever to be published in
the Soviet Union. In it, Progressors from the nearly utopian
twenty-first century planet Earth expect to guide the feudal
society of the planet Ankara along the path of historical
progress. The Earthling hero is perfectly disguised as a native
nobleman, outwardly adapting to the Ankaran life (a mixture of
medieval Europe and medieval Japan) in every detail, including
a native girlfriend. However, instead of following its projected
historical path of slow linear progress, the society of Ankara
veers off toward a fascist dictatorship, buttressed by an ignorant
and vulgar populace, and including specific features of Stalinism (identified by Darko Suvin as the "doctor's plot," stage-
managed confessions, recasting of history to exalt the present
ruler).[8] The Earthling "gods," powerful as they are in theory,
cannot undo Ankara's poverty and violence without forceful
intrusion. Since sparking a revolution and imposing a new dictatorship of any kind runs contrary to the Earthlings' humanistic principles, they are powerless to act. The hero is faced with
an acute ethical dilemma when the principle of noninterference
prevents him from acting, even when events lead to the killing
of the planet's leading intelligentsia and the Ankaran girl he
loves. For the first time in the Strugatskys' fiction, the path of
history and the path of ethical ideals obviously diverge. In
other words, the ethical and spiritual realm of human existence
is suddenly at odds with the sociopolitical realm. From now on,
what is "rendered unto Caesar" and what is "rendered unto
God" stand in stark opposition.

Later future history novels and the independent works written in the late sixties, seventies, and eighties paint an increasingly pessimistic picture of ethical and moral stagnation, where

the so-called vertical progress of history seems more like an absurd whirlpool funneling into an apocalyptic abyss. Without distinguishing between a middle and a late phase, we can simply refer to these novels as the "mature" works. A division between middle and late works cannot be made chronologically, since most of the "late" works that were not published until the liberal policy of glasnost took effect were actually written in the early 1970s.

The Inhabited Island (1969), *The Beetle in the Anthill* (1979), and *The Waves Still the Wind* (1985) form a trilogy which culminates the entire future history ("Progressorism") series. As Patrick McGuire has pointed out in his political analysis of the future history cycle, the face of international communism on Earth changes radically by the end of the series. In the final two novels, Maxim Kammerer, the former Progressor hero of *The Inhabited Island*, now works for the "Department of Extraordinary Events" under the auspices of the powerful Committee on Control. The combined acronyms of the two departments form an anagram for the notorious "Cheka," Stalin's secret police and forerunner of the KGB. In general,

> *Beetle* negates or contradicts much of the spirit of the works that came before it. COMCON . . . is nothing less than an organ of state coercion, and at that, one staffed by former covert operatives accustomed to working outside the law.
>
> Further, we are suddenly made aware of a mania for secrecy in the Strugatsky future society, though it faces no external threat save conceivably the super-advanced [alien] Wanderers. The only object of this secrecy can be to keep information out of the hands of the public— a public that has [supposedly] enjoyed full communism for two-and-a-half centuries![9]

Finally, in *The Waves Still the Wind*, the unifying plot motif of progressorism reaches a dead-end. By the year 2299, not only does Earth society apparently reject its former heroes, but the ex-Progressors themselves renounce their former calling:

> "Good is good!" Asya insisted.
> "You know perfectly well that that's not true. Or, maybe you really don't know? Even though I've explained [it] to you before. I was a Progressor for only three years, I brought good, only good, nothing but good, and Lord, how they hated me! It's fully understandable from their point of view. Because when the gods came, they came without

asking permission. Nobody invited them, but they came anyway and started to do good. That same good, which is always good. . . ."[10]

Within the philosophical context underlying the novels' construction (discussed in chapter 2), it is clear that the rejection of the notion that "good is always good" leads towards an exploration of the heterodoxical notion that evil, in the words of Goethe's Mephistopheles, is "that power which always wills evil, but eternally works good." Furthermore, it is clear that in the 22 years that have elapsed between the composition of *Hard to Be a God* and *The Waves Still the Wind,* the style and structure of the genre have undergone their own evolution. Despite its suggestive title, *Hard to Be a God* has no religious subtext. It very successfully adapts the straight adventure/historical novel form to the parabolic mode of science fiction. It is an "educational novel" insofar as the hero's adventures and the sociopolitical setting in which they take place can be seen as analogous to a historical or contemporary situation in the empirical world. In the 1964 novel the authors have little use for intertextual allusion, landscaped subtexts, or prefigurative motifs, all of which are essential stylistic and structural components of the mature novels to be discussed in the following chapters.

The Late Publications

In order to facilitate discussion of the Strugatskys late and untranslated novels, the somewhat convoluted history of their publication should be elucidated. The tug-of-war between hard-line conservative critics and liberal supporters (some of whom subsequently emigrated to Israel, confirming the conservatives' worst suspicions) over the Strugatskys' writing in the late sixties resulted in an uneasy truce, which lasted until the advent of glasnost in 1986. For a period of about eighteen years, some of the Strugatskys' works were published in numbers falling far short of the demand, and the rest of their work was not published at all. Although *The Ugly Swans* caused a scandal in 1972 when an unauthorized Russian edition and translation appeared in the West, few people knew that it was only one half of a larger novel the Strugatskys were working on called *A Lame Fate* (completed in 1984, published in 1986). *A Lame Fate* tells the partly autobiographical (on the basis of Arkady Strugatskys' reminiscences), partly fantastic story of a Soviet writer who does justice to his innermost convictions and conscience only in the unpublishable tale he writes "for the drawer": the text of *The Ugly Swans*. The common theme which ties the two parts together is the theme of Apocalypse. In different settings, both the frame story and the narrator's tale show how the structure and values of the present civilization have been discredited, but the face of the new civilization which prepares to rise in its place seems, for better or for worse, fundamentally alien.

The biggest surprise was the appearance of the novel *The Doomed City* in 1989 in the journal *Yunost*. The novel appeared to have been written on the crest of the new wave of glasnost and perestroika: it depicts animosity (in a "classless" society!) between rural and urban workers, bureaucrats, and the ruling elite; it depicts the growing hostility, in times of crisis, between different racial and ethnic groups; it depicts a catastrophic decline in cultural and linguistic norms; it depicts a successful coup by a fascist coalition which bases its authority over the multi-national city on the hypothetical presence of a hostile Anti-City. A statue reminiscent of both Peter the Great and Lenin at Finland Station stands confused at a crossroads in hell. A Chinese dissident blows himself up in a suicidal act of protest against the totalitarian regime. In the spring of 1989, none of these scenes seemed coincidental. Therefore, the impact of the outermost frame of the novel is considerable: the authors included the dates of the novel's composition as a *coda* to the story proper: *written in 1970-1972, 1975.*

The Strugatskys' latest full-length novel, *Burdened with Evil, or Forty Years Later,* was published in the journal *Yunost* in 1988. The structural and philosophical complexity of the novel does not lend itself to easy paraphrasing. In essence, the novel is the story of three Christs: the historical Jesus, his modern equivalent in the person of an enlightened and dedicated high school teacher, and the Demiurge, who embodies a gnostic interpretation of The Savior. The story is told from the point of view of the future, "forty years after" the end of the 20th century. The protagonist, a disciple of the teacher, interpolates his hagiography with chapters from a mysterious manuscript authored by the Demiurge's secretary during the time of the Demiurge's activity in the provincial Soviet town of Tashlinsk. The manuscript within the novel is spiced with noncanonical versions of Islamic history, Jewish history, as well as Stalinist history. The contemporary layers of the novel also depict modern-day leaders and disciples, in the guise of Soviet youth cults (Soviet hippies and punks).

According to the exhaustive bibliographical index prepared by an independent group of Strugatsky fans, excerpts and variants of *A Lame Fate* and *The Doomed City* appeared in regional journals before the novels were published as a whole in the leading "thick" journals. Furthermore, both *Burdened with Evil* and the two previously unpublished novels were immediately reprinted in full, in book form, by both State presses and by small cooperative publishing enterprises. A multi-volume edition of the Strugatskys' collected works is currently being prepared for publication by the private publishing firm Tekst.

Notes

1. *Zhidy goroda Pitera, ili neveselye besedy pri svechax. Komediia v dvukh deistviiakh* (Yids of the City of Peter, or Gloomy Discussions by Candlelight. A comedy in two acts), *Neva* 9 (1990): 92-115. The epigraph from Akutagawa is quoted from this play, p. 92.

2. Darko Suvin, *Metamorphoses of Science Fiction* (New Haven: Yale University Press, 1979), 6.

3. A case in point is the early reception of the Strugatskys' 1968 novella *The Snail on the Slope*. The unusual structure and surrealistic imagery of the novella constituted a dramatic break with the Strugatskys' previous, more conventional future history cycles, giving rise to many conflicting interpretations of the novella's "Forest" and "Administration" realms. In actuality, most of the Strugatskys' standard themes and structural oppositions remain intact in *The Snail on the Slope*, as discussed in chapter 4.

4. Mark Amusin, "Daleko li do budushchego?" *Neva* 2 (1988): 153.

5. Mikhail Lemkhin, "Tri povesti brat ev Strugatskikh" *Grani* 139 (1986): 92.

6. The earliest three novellas are *Strana bagrovykh tuch* (Land of the Crimson Clouds), 1959; *Put' na Amal'teiu* (Journey to Amalthea), 1960; and *Stazheri* (The Apprentices), 1962. The short stories appeared from 1959 to 1960 in monthly editions of the popular science journal *Znanie-sila;* thereafter, they were frequently anthologized.

7. The Strugatskys' most significant immediate predecessor in the science fiction genre was Ivan Efremov, who almost single-handedly resurrected the genre from its retreat into the safe confines of man-conquers-nature and/or imperialist enemies during the hegemony of "high" Socialist Realism, approx. 1934-54. The key to the Strugatskys' initial success and the essence of their departure from Efremov's precedent had to do with their stylistic "realism," as opposed to the stilted, neoclassical future heroes of Efremov's *Andromeda Nebula* (1956). The Strugatskys' future world had a "lived in" appearance.

8. Darko Suvin's introduction (pp. 1-20) to the English translation of *The Snail on the Slope* (Bantam Books, 1980) provides a brief and insightful overview of the Strugatskys' work up to 1968. *Hard to Be a God* was published separately without an introduction by DAW Books, Inc. (New York, 1973).

9. Patrick McGuire, "Future History, Soviet Style," in *Critical Encounters*, ed. Tom Staicer (New York, 1982), 121.

10. Arkady Strugatsky, and Boris Strugatsky, *Volni gasiat veter* (The Waves Still the Wind) (Haifa, Israel: N.p., 1986), 140-141.

Chapter One

Apocalyptic Realism

Genre

The Strugatskys' international reputation rests on their early debut as writers of science fiction. Critics who followed the Strugatskys' development through the sixties and seventies found it necessary to qualify the generic label in various ways in order to match the Strugatskys' diverse output with one or another point on the science fiction spectrum. Depending on which novel was under consideration, a case could be made for "philosophical fantasy," "sociopolitical satire," "inverted fairy tale,"[1] or, as the authors themselves suggested, "realistic fantasy." None of these labels is mutually exclusive, nor should they provoke a rebuttal. Except for the latter, they are simply irrelevant to the task at hand, which is to place the Strugatskys' mature works squarely into the context in which they are read.

From *within* the authors' and their native readers' world, the Strugatskys' work can be understood as yet another development in a distinguished line of Russian "realisms." Perhaps more than any other modern literature, Russian literature has sought to define itself for the last century and a half in terms of "realism." In Dostoevsky and Tolstoy, it saw a "Golden Age of Russian Realism." Furthermore, it has variously produced a so-called "psychological realism," a "critical realism," a (Soviet) "socialist realism," and, on the other hand, works of mystical revelation known as "illuminant realism."[2] To provide a more useful frame for an up-to-date analysis of the Strugatskys' work, I suggest that the Strugatskys' writing be called "apocalyptic realism" rather than science fiction.

In a fundamental way, the Strugatskys' mature work is shaped by their response to the apocalyptic literature of the Russian

Silver Age, and the "millenarian literature" of the 1920s' avant-garde. The Silver Age of Russian culture spanned roughly the last decade of the nineteenth century and the first two decades of the twentieth. The declining years of Tsarist Russia and the emergence of a new social order coincided with the spectacular flowering of Russian modernism in all the arts. In a relatively compressed period of artistic ferment radical innovations in music (Stravinsky's twelve-tone scale), and in the visual arts (Kandinsky, Chagall, Malevich) coincided with the rise and fall of a rich Symbolist tradition in poetry, which in turn was superseded by the poetic movements of Futurism and Acmeism. In prose literature, Andrei Bely, Fyodor Sologub, Valery Bryusov (to name a few) produced masterpieces of modernist fiction. Whereas the Silver Age bore witness to the end of an era, in the decade following the revolution, artists tried to make sense of the new age born of the cataclysmic events of 1917-1921 (Bolshevik Revolution and Civil War). Until the imposition of Socialist Realism as the single artistic mode in the 1930s, literature mirrored in theme and imagery the apocalyptic and millenarian fever which accompanied the birth of the new Soviet State.

Towards the end of his life, the Russian philosopher and religious thinker Nikolai Berdyaev summed up the essence of the Russian national character, as he perceived it, in a book called *The Russian Idea* (1946).[3] He stated that Russians are either apocalyptiscists or nihilists; thus, the "Russian Idea" is eschatological; it is oriented towards the end, and it is this which accounts for Russian maximalism. Such generalizations are important insofar as they reflect a society's mythical perception of itself—often transformed into a self-fulfilling prophesy. At least since the time of Peter I, Russian intellectuals have been occupied with defining their national identity in a land which occupies the crossroads of East and West, the old and the new, anarchy and authoritarianism, Orthodoxy and scientism. The binary oppositions by which Russia defines itself have always had a decidedly religious character—depending on one's orientation, one pole of any given opposition is equated with the antichrist, the other with universal salvation. (For example, Peter "the Great's" decision to open up Russia to the West convinced his opposition that the reign of the antichrist had arrived; just as many today associate Russia's transition to a market economy with swerving from the road of Orthodoxy and salvation). Accordingly, the Bolshevik Revolution in 1917 was perceived as the final confrontation in history between all oppositions; and Marxist-Leninism, no less than any overtly religious movement, promised the dawn of a utopian new age of universal brotherhood (communism in the "radiant future").

The importance of the "Russian Idea" (extremist and eschato-logical) to contemporary Russian literature, even when the Revolution's millenarian claims have long since become the punch line of sardonic jokes, is that it continues to survive and influence scientific, religious, and political culture. Another way of viewing this situation is provided by Lotman and Uspen-skii's structuralist model of cultural history:

> In Western Catholicism, the world beyond the grave is divided into three spaces: heaven, purgatory, and hell. Earthly life is correspond-ingly conceived of as admitting three types of behavior: the uncondi-tionally sinful, the unconditionally holy, and the neutral, which permits eternal salvation after some sort of purgative trial. In the real life of the medieval West a wide area of neutral behavior thus became possi-ble, as did neutral societal institutions, which were neither 'holy' nor 'sinful', neither 'pro-state' nor 'anti-state', neither good nor bad. [The Russian system, however] accented duality. . . . One of its attributes was the division of the other world into heaven and hell. Intermediate neutral spheres were not envisaged. . . . Duality and the absence of a neutral axiological sphere led to a conception of the new not as a con-tinuation, but as a total eschatological change.[4]

Lotman's and Uspenskii's structuralist scheme suggests an obvious binary structure for fictional literature dealing with Russian cultural myths about Russian national identity. Clearly, the conventional binary structure of science fiction can accommodate the oppositions of holy/sinful, old/new, east/ west, chaos/cosmos within its spatial, temporal and ethical formulas: Earth versus Outer Space, the Present versus the Future, and the Human versus the Alien. If this is so, then we might expect the Strugatskys to be able to use the science fic-tion paradigm to reexamine the philosophical, religious, and cultural heritage of Russia's modernist period.

The most basic underlying structure of all the Strugatskys' mature works is described by two axes suggested in the generalizations above, and the hypothetical axes take as their zero point the sociopolitical event of the Revolution and the founding of the Soviet State. This moment was supposed to divide history into two periods: the exploitative and degenerate old world was to be transformed into a new, proletarian paradise. The Strugatskys do not reverse this vector to claim that the old world was better than the new; they simply describe contemporary, everyday life in the Soviet Union as appallingly banal, bureaucratic, imperfect, and spiritually bankrupt. This layer of their prose is always recognizable, whether or not the action is explicitly set in the contemporary Soviet Union (e.g., Leningrad in *One Billion Years Before the End of the World;* Moscow in *A Lame Fate;* or the fictional "Tashlinsk," in *Burdened with Evil)* or in some more abstract location (on another planet; in abstract time/space). Thus, a characteristic feature of the Strugatskys' science fiction is the use of specific, recognizable, everyday detail to evoke a setting. Likewise, characters' speech patterns and mannerisms are purposely modern and colloquial, corresponding to recognizable contemporary types rather than to ostensible future or extra-terrestrial culture. We might posit a horizontal axis of description which runs the gamut of the mundane aspects of a Soviet citizen's contemporary existence. This axis should properly be called the axis of *byt.* "*Byt*" is an untranslatable Russian term meaning, roughly, the dull, routine, hopeless dreariness which inheres in the physical reality of one's everyday life. Long lines are part of *byt.* Simple appliances that don't work are part of *byt.* A dye lot of objectionable, ugly deep orange which determines the color of all available curtains and upholstery for five years is part of *byt.* Clearly, much of the Strugatskys' irony is aimed at the sorry condition of the "new millennium." If the Revolution signalled the end of history, than what has followed is not the Kingdom of Heaven, but its ludicrous parody: contemporary *byt.*

However, the starting point of the Russian Revolution is also crossed by another, vertical axis. This axis is best understood as an unbroken continuum of cultural memory. That is, a succession of literary styles, philosophical trends, historical events, and religious debates which had been suppressed by the regime and largely forgotten during the Strugatskys' lifetime is pieced back together by way of frequent symbolic or intertextual allusion. As the preliminary work for this study progressed, it became increasingly evident that a significant source of meaning and imagery in the Strugatskys' "future" or "alien" worlds is derived from the literary and philosophical/religious heritage of Russia's Silver Age and post-Revolutionary avant-garde. The authors' intertextual allusions to Bulgakov, Bely, Platonov, and the Russian Absurdists *(Oberiu* poets) represent a conscious effort to respond to the theme of apocalypse present in Russian literature during the immediate pre- and post-Revolutionary era. Furthermore, the Strugatskys, like their Silver Age and 1920s predecessors, attempt to redefine the relevance of Judeao-Christian apocalyptic thought to contemporary Russian life by incorporating into their fantastic world imagery from the gnostic and Manichaean heresies, the cosmology of Dante, and—of course—the biblical Revelation.

The coincidence of allusions to Bulgakov's Margarita and the Divine Sophia, of Bely's *Petersburg* and Manichaean dualism, of Platonov's *Foundation Pit* and Dante's *Inferno* also suggest the influence of Vladimir Solovyov and Nikolai Fyodorov on the shape of the Strugatskys' science fiction from the 1970s on. Generally speaking, both Solovyov and Fyodorov based their eschatologies on a distinctly Russian interpretation of the meaning of Christianity. Fyodorov, in particular, sought a grand synthesis of scientific rationalism and mystical idealism. The long-suppressed teachings of Fyodorov were newly coming into vogue among the Russian intelligentsia during the post-thaw period. Writing on the crest of this wave of interest, the Strugatskys seem to incorporate elements of "Fyodorovian" utopianism into their depictions of the "alien." It is not always possible, or indeed necessary, to pinpoint the source of a motif to a specific text, especially in times when certain ideas are "in the air," and freely used in many different contexts. This is particularly true of various manifestations of gnostic thought which appear in Fyodorov's teachings as well as in the novels of Bely and Bulgakov, but could also have been gleaned by the Strugatskys from other scholarly sources. In any case, they are among the first post-war Russian writers to retrieve this important thread of Russian culture and give it new literary shape.

In short, one finds that fantastic images in the Strugatskys' late works are taken neither from the high-tech realm of cybernetics, nor from magical world of the fairy tale. Rather, they draw their images from the metaphysical systems of the early Christian heresies and dualist cosmologies, and the incorporation of these systems into the Russian modernist movement at the beginning of this century. Therefore, their genre is clearly distinct from the science fantasies of Stanislaw Lem, or—at the opposite pole—from the Christian fantasies of C. S. Lewis. It is also distinct from the so-called "magic realism" of the Latin American school.

What are the specific devices which characterize the Strugatskys' "apocalyptic realism"? Before discussing the late novels individually, it is necessary to look at how the hypothetical axes we have proposed—the axis of *byt* and the axis of cultural memory—intersect on the levels of plot, setting, and characterization.

Plot

One way in which the Strugatskys began to increase the complexity of their fiction was to incorporate the philosophical and metaphysical issues they wished to address as elements of the plot. Whether consciously or not, the authors developed a form which would let the nature of the extra-textual or intertextual material actually affect and predetermine the course of events in what was ostensibly a purely entertaining, action-packed plot. Once this was achieved, the science fiction, detective, or adventure story plot was not merely a vehicle for allegory; rather, it could in some way be shaped and anticipated by the underlying philosophical agenda.

The particular literary device which evolved in the Strugatskys work in the 1980s is the device of *plot prefiguration*. The term "prefiguration" was originally coined from a translation of the Latin *figura,* which was used to describe the scheme whereby "the persons and events of the Old Testament were prefigurations of the New Testament and its history of Salvation."[5] In its secularized sense the term includes a much broader range of anticipatory patterns, such as the use of a classical myth, a Shakespeare play, or a Superman comic strip as a motif which can prefigure and hence anticipate the plot of an original literary work in a number of different ways.

In his study of plot prefiguration, John J. White views the device of prefiguration in literature as part of a modern "rhetoric of fiction," which evolved in the twentieth century in correlation with the development of theoretical (and fashionable) constraints on the use of direct authorial comment in the novel.[6] If the author uses a well-known motif to pattern and anticipate the modern plot, then any deviations, changes, or additions to the underlying pattern are inherently meaningful. Moreover, once the reader has discerned the beginnings of a recognizable pattern of allusions, a set of expectations is activated about what can possibly happen as the plot develops further and the prefigurative motif is adhered to. In this regard, the location and context in which bits of the prefigurative motif occur is more important than the frequency of their occurrence. In all of the relevant Strugatsky works, it can be shown that the relative infrequency and inconsistency of allusions to the prefigurative motif is counter-balanced by their appearance at decisive moments in the plot, and by their relevance to the underlying philosophical themes in the novels. In other words, the prefigurative motif does not function as a structural scaffold to be fleshed out by the modern plot, e.g., it is not necessary for a character whose life is prefigured by the life of Christ to function as a *imitatio Christi*. Rather, it is a means of providing a symbolic commentary on certain events and characters; it offers a familiar analogy to help the reader understand the modern (or future) situation described in the novel.

The Strugatskys seem to find particular advantage in using literary prefiguration in their future history series. This is not surprising, since in a series the plot of each successive novel is already somewhat determined by the preceding novel, and one way to allow an old plot to take on new meaning is to juxtapose it with a prefigured pattern. *The Beetle in the Anthill* and *The Waves Still the Wind*, the last two novels of a future history trilogy, were written a decade after the first novel of the trilogy. Evidently, the Strugatskys intended to continue the popular adventure plot of the first novel, but the metaphysical and scientific issues which preoccupied them at the time found their way into a second layer of meaning provided by the prefigurative motif.

In another instance of plot prefiguration—this time from *Burdened with Evil*, the obscurity of the prefigurative text causes the function of the device to be reversed. Instead of being able to recognize and anticipate a pattern, the reader must resort to an encyclopedia to find the historical basis for the an episode in the plot. Nevertheless, all three prefigurative texts feature the appearance of a false prophet, a quintessential figure in times of apocalyptic foreboding.

Setting

The Strugatskys' use of the setting *as a topographical embodiment of ideas* is the single most important device which enables them to mediate between the realistic and the fantastic layers of narration. In Soviet mainstream literature of the seventies and eighties, there was a trend towards detailed description of the mundane aspects of everyday life. While everyone outside of the accepted literary establishment—from emigre and dissident writers such as Aksyonov, Sinyavsky and Aleshkovsky to second-rate science fiction hacks—was producing fantastic and phantasmagorical works, the mainstream prose writers of the seventies by and large eschewed elements of the fantastic and the grotesque. Socialist realism, it seemed, had given way to a more critical and more sober "urban realism." This trend was somewhat reversed in 1981 with the death of the most outstanding "urban prose" writer, Iurii Trifonov, and the publication of Chingiz Aitmatov's *The Day Lasts Longer Than a Century*, a novel hailed for bringing science fiction elements into the mainstream. The Strugatskys' development shows a reverse course.

Starting with the 1976 novel *One Billion Years Before the End of the World*, the Strugatskys move away from abstract and intergalactic settings in order to concentrate on the here and now. However, the contemporary, mundane setting of Soviet *byt* is also used as a symbolic repository of literary and cultural allusions. The trick is to create a double-vision of the modern age:

"realistic" depictions of contemporary Soviet life reveal a banal and godless landscape, while symbolic motifs within that landscape point to its true location somewhere on the battleground between Christ and the antichrist (where the antichrist, for the time being, has successfully established an anti-millennium!). Frances A. Yates' fascinating study of the classical, medieval, and Renaissance *Art of Memory* provides the most useful theoretical context in which to analyze the unusual relationship between setting and theme in the Strugatskys' science fiction. [7]

In the classical world, before the invention of the printing press, the ability to store in proper order a large or complicated set of information was of utmost importance to any intellectual endeavor. An accomplished orator of could recite lengthy speeches without the use of notes; a lawyer in Greek or Roman antiquity could keep innumerable facts about a case straight in his head; Augustine claimed to have a friend who could recite Virgil backwards. [8] Leaving aside for the moment the question of why somebody would want to recite Virgil backwards, we should understand what kind of mnemotechnics the ancients used to achieve a prodigious "artificial memory."

It was considered that the natural memory could be greatly expanded and enhanced by attaching an image of the thing to be memorized to a place. For instance, the image of a weapon prompts the passage in a speech having to do with military matters; an anchor reminds the speaker of the passage concerning nautical matters. The weapon and the anchor, along with as many other images as there are notions in the speech, are "placed" in the speaker's mind onto a series of well-known locations in the following manner:

> The first step was to imprint on the memory a series of *loci*, or places. The commonest, though not the only, type of mnemonic place system used was the architectural type. The clearest description of the process is that given by Quintilian [Rome, first century, A.D.]. In order to form a series of places in memory, he says, a building is to be remembered, as spacious and varied a one as possible, the forecourt, the living room, bedrooms, and parlours, not omitting statues and other ornaments with which the rooms are decorated. The images by which the speech is to be remembered—as an example of these Quintilian says one may use an anchor or a weapon—are then placed in imagination on the places which have been memorized in the building. This done,

as soon as the memory of the facts requires to be revived, all these places are visited in turn and the various deposits demanded of their custodians. We have to think of the ancient orator as moving in imagination through his memory building whilst he is making his speech, drawing from the memorized places the images he has placed on them. This method ensures that the points are remembered in the right order, since the order is fixed by the sequence of places in the building. (Yates, 3)

This basic procedure for aiding the memory can also make use of fictitious, rather than actual *loci*. It is enough to conjure up an interior or exterior setting in one's imagination, as long as it provides a uniquely ordered, vivid pattern of *loci* which can "harbor" the necessary images until they need to be recalled.

Interestingly enough, what evolves in the classical world as a means for improving one's rhetorical skills is shifted by the medieval scholastics into the realm of ethics. One of the four virtues—Prudence, is defined as consisting of three parts: *memoria, intelligentia, providentia*. Thus, the cultivation of artificial memory in the Middle Ages became part of the exercise of Prudence (Yates, 54, 55). However, when the voices of the orators were silenced in the authoritarian culture of the Middle Ages, the art of memory for rhetorical purposes was no longer necessary, and rapidly forgotten. Charlemagne's call to Alcuin to come to France to help restore the educational system of antiquity sounds today like an echo of the contemporary need to restore lost and distorted cultural memory:

Charlemagne: What, now, are you to say about Memory, which I deem to be the noblest part of rhetoric?
Alcuin: What indeed unless I repeat the words of Marcus Tullius [Cicero] that 'Memory is the treasure-house of all things and unless it is made custodian of the thought-out things and words, we know that all the other parts of the orator, however distinguished they may be, will come to nothing.'
Charlemagne: Are there not other precepts which tell us how it can be obtained or increased?
Alcuin: We have no other precepts about it, except exercise in memorizing, practice in writing, application to study, and the avoidance of drunkenness which does the greatest possible injury to all good studies.[9]

A consistent theme in all of the Strugatskys' mature works is the catastrophic loss of cultural memory which has occurred in the Soviet Union within their lifetime. In the Strugatskys' handling, the genre of science fiction itself is subordinate to this theme, since a culture which cannot remember its past cannot "remember" its future, either. The Strugatskys' non-extrapolatory science fiction is based on the notion that the rapid loss of cultural memory has shortened the approach of the future, which, in fact, has already merged with the present. The stylistic result of this conflation of the present with an unimaginable and unimagined future is most noticeable in the description of the setting.

As we shall see in more detail, the Strugatskys' settings provide the *loci* and the images to jog one's memory of a long and complicated subtext—the Western cultural heritage of the Russian intelligentsia. The settings of all the novels discussed in this chapter are intentionally—to the point of stylistic didacticism—designed as fictional "rooms" or "landscapes" cluttered with half-familiar "images" which represent the concepts and the texts the authors wish the reader to recall. The most primitive and direct use of this device is evident, for example, in *Burdened with Evil*, when one of the narrator's rooms is hung with a painting signed by "Adolf Schickelgruber" (Hitler's real name). Hitler himself is not mentioned in the text or in the plot *per se,* but the influence of his ideological presence is noted. In *The Doomed City*, the protagonist's daily walk home to the suburbs leads him past workers digging a foundation pit. At the same time, the reader must mentally "walk by" Platonov's novel *The Foundation Pit;* i.e., the device insures that the reader will recall both the content of Platonov's long-suppressed anti-utopian masterpiece, and its proper "location" (order) in the broken and distorted continuum of Russian intellectual history. In the setting of *The Waves Still the Wind* examined in the next chapter, the text of the Revelation of Saint John is imprinted upon the landscape. In *The Doomed City* and *A Lame Fate*, landscapes and interiors harbor the imagery of a rich and eclectic selection of the literary and philosophical "monuments to the spirit" inherited by the Russian intelligentsia at the turn of the century. A closer examination of these settings is crucial, since it should reveal exactly what part of Russia's cultural memory is being sculpted into the literary landscape for preservation, and why.

Characterization

How are the apocalyptic and gnostic motifs underlying plot formation and sculpted into the landscape reflected in the characterization of the protagonists? How does the relationship between the human protagonist and the alien change over time? The study of characterization culminates the process of discovering how the Strugatskys' unique brand of science fiction has served the needs of the Russian intelligentsia so well for three full decades. One might expect that the intelligentsia readership has found a reflection of itself in the Strugatskys' heroes, and this is indeed the case. Furthermore, by using the fantastic license to model reality, the authors have actually provided the intelligentsia with more than a reflection; they have provided a kind of cultural myth to live by. The Strugatskys' heroes not only embody the values of the intelligentsia at any given time; they carry these values into the experimental future or alternative world of the fantastic, where they find either rejection or affirmation.

So far, we have predicted that a prefigurative plot or a "loaded" landscape can refer the educated reader to a variety of other texts which are important for cultural memory. The pattern of subtexts discovered by the reader lends considerable philosophical depth to the superficially straight-forward, popular-genre format. Clearly, the more the reader knows about the inter-textual world the Strugatskys refer to, the greater the meaning (and didactic value) of the novel. A reader less literate in the cultural experience of the Russian/Jewish intellectual in the twentieth-century Soviet Union will understand the novel accordingly: as a more or less self-referential, purely fictional entertainment. Before connecting this aspect of reader-reception to the "myth-making" function of the Strugatskys' science fiction, it is necessary to look at the more obscure subtexts which inform and change the image of the hero in the late works.

The earliest "typical" hero of the Strugatskys' science fiction is a devout believer in the power of Reason; specifically, in its application towards scientific progress and education of the masses. However, these gentle heroes of the Khrushchev period are not rational robots, but champions of a new, more rational society—one which will finally achieve the humanistic socialist goals that were "temporarily" betrayed by Stalin's "Cult of Personality." Their utopian sociopolitical ideals and impeccable ethical code of behavior notwithstanding, the ever-popular early Strugatsky heroes of *Far Rainbow* (1963), *Hard to Be a God* (1964) and *Monday Begins on Saturday* (1965) are not lacking in humor, ironic wit, and endearing eccentricities.

In the Strugatskys' earliest phase, roughly coinciding with the first half of the 60s decade, their optimistic scientist-heroes reflect the optimism of the scientific intelligentsia favored (at first) by the Khrushchevian reforms. In the next phase, roughly coinciding with the next decade, the intelligentsia's renewed access to the philosophy of Nikolai Fyodorov and the legacy of the Silver Age's fascination with occult and mystical systems is reflected in the characterization of women, children, and super-human aliens. Therefore, chapter 4 will take a closer look at the pattern of literary and cultural subtexts which shape the characterization of the "Other." The most striking aspect of the future world represented by the alien protagonists is the avowedly anti-humanistic, neo-platonic or gnostic tradition it embodies.

It is possible to distinguish the features of a third type of protagonist in the Strugatskys' mature works. The alternative to the naive socialist humanist and the dangerous mystical idealist is embodied in the figure of the Wandering Jew. The Wandering Jew has none of the illusions of the socialist utopian, but in spite of his profound pessimism, he has enough faith (ironically) to reject the scientific and mystical synthetic solutions offered by the "false prophets." He is characterized as a figure of infinite endurance, eternally persecuted, but eternally holding on to his sense of humor and cultural history.

Notes

1. See Istvan Csicsery-Ronay, "Towards the Last Fairy Tale: On the Fairy Tale Paradigm in the Strugatskys' Science Fiction: 1963-1972," *Science Fiction Studies* 13 (1986): 1 41.

2. Daniil Andreev, in *Rosa Mira* (The Rose of the World), refers to works of the Russian Symbolists at the turn of this century as creations of "illuminant realism" ("skvoziashchii realizm"), where symbolic images allow what is real (in Andreev s understanding) to illuminate our world, like light shining through a chink in the doorway.

3. Nikolai Berdiaev, *Russkaia Ideia* (Paris: YMCA Press, 1946). Berdyaev (1874-1948) emigrated from Russia in 1922. Berdyaev's writings on the philosophy of religion, ethics, and history, based on his concept of freedom and the human personality, are enjoying a new vogue in post-glasnost Russia.

4. Iurii Lotman and Boris Uspenskii, "Binary Models in the Dynamics of Russian Culture," *The Semiotics of Russian Cultural History*, eds. A. D. and A. S. Nakhimovsky (Ithaca: Cornell University Press, 1985), 32.

5. Erich Auerbach, *"Figura* in the Phenomenal Prophecy of the Church Fathers," *Scenes from the Drama of European Literature* (New York: 1959), 30.

6. The theoretical discussion of literary prefiguration is based on John J. White's *Mythology in the Modern Novel: A Study of Prefigurative Techniques* (Princeton University Press, 1971), and Theodore Ziolkowski's *Fictional Transfigurations of Jesus* (Princeton University Press, 1972).

7. Francis A. Yates, *The Art of Memory* (University of Chicago Press, 1966).

8. Yates, 16.

9. W. S. Howell, *The Rhetoric of Charlemagne and Alcuin* (Princeton and Oxford: 1941), 136.

Chapter Two

False Prophets

The Pied Piper

The Beetle in the Anthill appeared in serial form at the end of 1979 and the beginning of 1980 in the journal *Znanie-sila.* It continues the future history cycle inaugurated several years earlier with the publication of *The Inhabited Island.* The two novels are so different in style and tone, that they need not be considered together.[1]

The Beetle in the Anthill consists of Maxim Kammerer's journal entries, ostensibly written over a four-day period in June, [21]78, and a story-within-the-story, which consists of excerpts from a report presented to Maxim by one of his former employees in the summer of [21]63. The frame narration records Maxim's efforts to track down his former employee, one Lev Abalkin, who has illegally returned to Earth after eighteen years of professional activity on explored and unexplored planets of the Periphery. Maxim's immediate superior, the chief of Earth's powerful Committee on Control ("COMCON"), has reason to believe that Abalkin is a humanoid—but non-human—agent planted by the supercivilization of the Wanderers in the "anthill" of humanity in order to carry out some unfathomable experiment. Prior to the drama which unfolds in the novel, Abalkin had considered himself a man exiled to professional activity in the Periphery unfairly. Now, his clandestine return to Earth indicates that he has become aware of his non-human identity and presumably anti-human mission. Maxim's journal describes the Committee's top-secret, murderous attempt to hunt Abalkin down before its dire but vague and unproved suspicions are confirmed. The plot is complicated by the fact that Maxim himself is left in the dark as to why

Abalkin's whereabouts is a matter of such urgent concern. In *The Beetle in the Anthill,* the frame narration is constructed as a spy thriller: as pieces of the puzzle fall into place, the tension builds toward a climactic shoot-out described in the last entry of Maxim's journal.

The imbedded story, on the other hand, stands apart from the forward movement of the plot as a self-contained piece in the genre of science fiction. It describes a single day of reconnaissance work on the nearly-deserted planet Hope. The reconnaissance team is headed by Maxim's former subordinate, the same Lev Abalkin, then an up-and-coming young "xeno-zoopsychologist," and the first person to work successfully with a member of a non-humanoid race. Abalkin's partner Shchokn is a representative of the "Golovans," a race of highly intuitive, articulate, but irascible canines. The imbedded story is an eye-witness report of the planet Hope operation, written by Abalkin's hand, and preserved in Maxim's files. It is presented in three installments, providing material for chapters seven, thirteen, and eighteen—roughly one-quarter of the novel. Maxim's narration, on the other hand, presents the *official* theory on the collapse of planet Hope's civilization:

> Fifteen years ago the planet Hope and its horrible fate was a hot topic much discussed on Earth. . . . It has now been firmly established that in the final century of their civilization, the inhabitants of Hope lost all control over the development of their technology and irreversibly destroyed the planet's ecological balance. Nature was ruined. Industrial wastes and refuse from the absurd, desperate experiments undertaken in an attempt to rectify the situation befouled the planet to such a degree, that the local race of humans fell prey to a whole complex of genetic disorders, and was simply doomed to complete degeneration and inevitable extinction. Gene structures on the planet Hope had gotten out of control . . . and then the Wanderers arrived. As far as we know, this was the first time that they actively interfered in the affairs of another world. It has now been firmly established that they managed to evacuate the great majority of the planet's inhabitants through interspace tunnels, and, it seems, save them (187).[2]

Abalkin's report provides a different perspective, straight from the mouth of one of the few remaining survivors of the planet's mass destruction and evacuation:

It turns out that everything is to blame on a race of repulsive non-people inhabiting the bowels of the planet. About four decades ago that race launched an attack on the local human population. The attack began with an unprecedented pandemic, with which the non-people infected the whole planet at once. . . .

The pandemic raged for three years before the non-people first announced their existence. They presented each of our governments with a proposal to organize a transfer of the population to a "neighboring world," that is, to their world, in the bowels of the earth. They promised that there, in the neighboring world, the pandemic would spontaneously disappear. So millions of frightened people threw themselves into special wells, from which, of course, nobody has ever returned. That s how the local civilization disappeared forty years ago. (272)

The official theory describes a classic science fiction catastrophe scenario with a fairy-tale happy ending; whereas, the eyewitness report is a kind of evil fairy-tale with a real-life, historical subtext. Maxim's journal is dated in the year of '78; planet Hope's fate was a "hot topic" fifteen years earlier, in '63; and the actual purging of the planet's population took place forty years before, in '38. The significance of these dates in twentieth-century Soviet history is not lost on the reader: 1938 was the peak year of Stalin's purges; 1963 was the last year of the short-lived Khrushchevian thaw, when Stalin's crimes were openly discussed; but by 1978, Brezhnev's reactionary regime was once again insisting upon certain "firmly established" falsifications of history. The novel is full of cabalic numbers and names which have been deciphered by one emigre critic to a single cryptic motif: "The fate of the Jews is examined by the authors in the light . . . of two catastrophes, one of which has already occurred [Nazi Germany], and the other which is still to come [Nationalistic Russia]" (Kaganskaia, 173).[3] The authors themselves have taken issue with Kaganskaia's interpretation (in private conversation, 1989), claiming that it reads significance into names and dates which are simply necessary for plot coherence. The truth may well lie somewhere in between: the Strugatskys certainly intended to write more than a fast-paced spy thriller set in the twenty-second century, but their subtext is broader than the Jewish question alone, and the key to the novel's sociopolitical dimension must be found in the structure of the plot as well as in symbolic dates.

The legend of the Pied Piper determines to a significant degree the characters, imagery, and sequence of events which comprise Abalkin's planet Hope report. As Abalkin and Shchokn are making their way slowly across the desolate urban wasteland of one of Hope's main cities, searching for clues to the cause of an entire civilization's sudden collapse, a jester appears. The appearance of a dancing, brightly-clothed harlequin is so out-of-keeping with the science fiction "reality" of this post-holocaust world, that even the narrator notes a certain generic incompatibility:

> A jester. A harlequin. His antics would probably be funny, if they weren't so frightful in this dead city. . . . (208)

However, the jesters on planet Hope share many of the most important features attributed to the Pied Piper in hundreds of literary reworkings of the legend. The first jester Abalkin and Shchokn meet is characterized as

> skinny as a skeleton, sallow-faced, with sunken cheeks and a glazed look in his eyes. His wet red locks of hair stick out in all directions, he flails about his seemingly multi-jointed arms, and his lanky legs jerk and dance without stop, so that putrid leaves and sodden cement gravel fly out from under his enormous feet.
>
> He is dressed from head to foot in some kind of fabric with multi-colored checkers—red, yellow, blue, and green, and [his] little bells jingle constantly. . . . (208)

This image of the Piper derives in part from the association sometimes made between the legend of the Pied Piper and the historical phenomenon of St. Vitus' dance. It has been speculated that entranced victims of the medieval *Tanzwut* might have followed a "piper" out of town. The Strugatskys' mad jester seems to be a conflation of the plague-ridden dancers *and* the brightly clothed, devilish musician who claims to lead people out of the plague. If the specter of the Pied Piper exists on the Strugatskys' planet Hope, so do the rats. "There are a lot of rats," notes Abalkin on the first page of his report,

> [I hear] sounds of scuffling, squeals, crunching, and slurping. Shchokn reappears in the doorway. He's chewing energetically and wiping rat tails from his chops. (207)

The legend of the Pied Piper supplies more than imagery and characterization; its structure prefigures the structure of events in Abalkin's story. The legend's plot paradigm consists of a) a city plagued by rats; b) an itinerant rat-catcher who promises to relieve the city for a certain reward; c) he accomplishes his task by leading the rats away with the music of his pipe; d) the citizenry denies him his promised reward; e) the Piper leads the city's children with his irresistible tune away to a nearby mountain, where they all disappear forever, without a trace.[4]

Reduced to its bare structure, the story of planet Hope evolves as follows: a) a planet falls victim to a decimating plague; b) an unknown supercivilization proposes to lead Hope's citizens away into a new, clean world; c) most of the planet's population is evacuated through the supercivilization's interspace tunnel; d) armed minority factions resist the evacuation and fight to protect their own, albeit plague-ridden civilization to the bitter end; e) the supercivilization contrives to lure the city s remaining children into its unfathomable other world.

(a) In the archetypical legend, the rats and the plague are simply a fact of life, neither God's scourge nor Nature's punishment. In the Strugatskys' version, the origin of the plague is directly linked to the irresponsible, dangerous greed and blindness of a technologically ambitious society (Maxim's "official" version); or to the malevolent will of an alien, external power (survivor's version). The structural device of placing a story within a story, i.e., Abalkin's report as a separate part within Maxim's narration, allows the two interpretations to overlap. The double moral is as obvious as it is pessimistic: technological advancement is dangerous not only in and of itself, but in conjunction with social and psychological backwardness, it carries with it the seeds of another holocaust: the same society that is capable of creating a ruinous technology is capable of blaming an alien "race of disgusting non-people" for its own failures.

(b) In the Strugatskys' version, the supercivilization functions as the Piper, who promises to lead the populace to a place where there is no plague.

(c) In the Brothers' Grimm version of the legend, the rats follow the Piper out of the city into the river Weser, where they
drown.   Robert Browning's famous poem embellishes this
sequence of events with the metaphor of an army marching:

> And ere three shrill notes the pipe uttered,
>   You heard as if an army muttered;
>   And the muttering grew to grumbling;
> And the grumbling grew to a mighty rumbling;
> And out of the houses the rats came tumbling . . .

and with the anthropomorphization of the rat families:

>   Families by tens and dozens,
>   Brothers, sisters, husbands, wives -
>   Followed the Piper for their lives.
>   . . .
>   Until they came to the river Weser,
>   Wherein all plunged and perished![5]

Both of Browning's poetic metaphors—the army, and the
"brothers, sisters, husbands, wives" following "for their
lives"—are actualized in the Strugatskys' science fiction version.
It is at this point in the text that the Pied Piper motif overlaps
with the empirical historical source guiding the narrator's
choice of images.   Like the rats in Browning's poem, the families of planet Hope followed their "pipers" as an army of evac-
uees—but this army has a specific twentieth-century precedent:
the evacuation of the Jews to death camps during the holocaust.
Abalkin's report contains an eerie scene of *deja vu.*

> I don't even need a search light anymore to see that the asphalt here is
> almost completely covered by a rather thick, unappetizing crust of
> some kind of moist, compressed matter, abundantly overgrown with
> variously colored molds. I take out my knife and poke the surface of
> this crust—and something like a rag, or a piece of a strap peels away
> from the crust. . . .
>   I stand up and proceed further, stepping across the soft and slip-
> pery surface. I try to contain my imagination, but it doesn't work. All
> of them went this way, along this very road, abandoning their big cars
> and vans, hundreds of thousands and millions [of people] poured from
> the boulevard onto this square, circumventing the tank with its threat-
> ening, but pointlessly directed machine guns. They walked, dropping
> the few things they had tried to take with them. . . . For some reason, it

seems as though all of this happened at night, this human kasha was illuminated by a deathly, deceptive light, and it was quiet, as in a dream. . . .

"A hole..." says Shchokn.

I turn on the search light. There is no hole. . . . but just in ahead of us gleams a large—about twenty by forty—wet black square of naked asphalt.

" Steps!" says Shchokn, as if in despair. "They're full of holes! Deep! I can't see. . . ."

Shivers run up and down my spine: I have never heard Shchokn speak in such a strange voice. (235)

The "hole" which the extraordinarily intuitive Shchokn fears like death itself appears to Abalkin as simply a black square. The black square also symbolizes the door to a gas chamber in an earlier Strugatsky novel, *The Snail on the Slope* (see p. 133).

(d) In the legend, the *kleinbürgerliche* citizens of Hamelin deny the Pied Piper his promised reward for ridding the city of rats. In *The Beetle in the Anthill*, this pivotal moment is almost entirely absent, for the simple reason that although the Wanderers "actively interfered" in the affairs of planet Hope, there is no implication that they demanded a reward. This is the single most significant departure from the Pied Piper subtext, since it rules out any easy moral: no promises were broken, no reward offered and then rescinded by the stingy, narrow-minded townsfolk. On the contrary, a fierce resistance to the Wanderers' evacuation plan is launched for moral and ethical reasons. The words of one of the survivors Abalkin meets do not belong to a complacent middle class, but to an embattled dissident minority, distinguished not by the color of its skin or social class, but by its world view:

Of course, not everybody believed [in the supercivlization's promise], and not everybody let themselves be frightened. Whole families and groups of families remained, [banding together as] whole religious communities. In the monstrous conditions of the pandemic, they continued their hopeless battle for existence and for the right to live as their ancestors had lived. However, the non-people did not even leave that miserable percentage of the former population in peace. They organized a veritable hunt for the children, that last hope of humanity. (273)

(e) The supercivilization, or "non-people," as Hope's natives refer to them, respond to the native population's resistance as in the archetypical legend: they begin to lure all the children away. According to the survivor, colorful, bell-jangling jesters were conjured up by the "non-people" to abduct the children. This reconfirms our original assumption that the mad jester on planet Hope is "prefigured" by the Pied Piper legend. In this version, moreover, he functions as a quintessentially evil Piper. He abducts innocent children, wreaking vengeance on a minority faction of heroic resistors. He does so without the justification he has in the legend, where the city leaders have gone back on their promise to him.

Abalkin's reaction to the eye-witness' account forestalls the reader's own reaction to the contradictory evidence presented in different layers of the text and subtext, and provides further instructions on how the story should be read:

> Subconsciously I had expected something like [the survivor's story], but what I heard from an eye-witness and a victim still will not fit into my comprehension. The facts the old man gave me don't elicit any doubt, but—it's like in a dream: each element taken separately makes sense, but everything taken together looks like complete absurdity. Maybe the problem is that I have too thoroughly assimilated some kind of prejudiced notion of the Wanderers, which is accepted without question on Earth? (274)

Abalkin's admission that he shares a generally accepted prejudice against the alien race provides one more piece in the pattern of allusions to the "Jewish question." However, like many of the other "loaded" images and allusions in the story, its meaning does not inhere in the science fiction plot or character which carries it. Clearly, the Wanderers do not systematically represent a supercivilization which frightens the citizens to stampede to their death, nor do they systematically represent a persecuted alien race. Rather, the true course of history in the Strugatskys' generation—which was routinely, officially distorted—is now fragmented into its component parts and displaced onto a well-known prefigurative motif, the legend of the Pied Piper. The underlying prefiguration, in turn, provides a basis for meaningful comparison and contrast with the science fiction plot it to some degree controls. The prefigurative motif provides a kind of "conductor surface," through which information from the "real world" can impinge on the fantasy world of the popular genre.

The logic and imagery of the science fiction story alone in *The Beetle in the Anthill* would require a happy ending. According to this logic, the responsible adult population and their government leaders were to blame for the ecological and moral decay of an entire planet. Representatives of a supercivilization interfered in the hopeless situation of this plague-ridden planet and transported all the children under twelve (still physically, and, by implication, spiritually healthy) into another world, a new "Hope." However, the logic and imagery of the Pied Piper motif, superimposed upon the historical experience of Soviet intellectuals and Jews in the Strugatskys' generation, leads to a tragic outcome, epitomized by the gruesome human deportation and abduction of children described in (c) and (e).

The Strugatskys' adaptation and transformation of the Pied Piper legend in *The Beetle in the Anthill* successfully exploits the ambiguity between the tragic and the fairy tale possibilities of the legend. There are two possible conclusions to the imbedded story. One might say that the children are lucky to escape the ecologically devastated and morally befouled world their parents inhabit. The other conclusion is that they are being lured away from their own humanity into another, alien civilization which is by definition evil. Both positions are tenable, although they are mutually exclusive. The moral judgment call the reader makes on the tragic denouement of the frame story (a spy thriller) is determined by which of the two positions he or she adopts.[6]

The Revelation

The Waves Still the Wind followed *The Beetle on the Anthill* as the third and final novel of the trilogy involving Maxim Kammerer and his activity in the COMCON organization.

In *The Waves Still the Wind*, Maxim Kammerer's narration is structured as a detective story. The protagonist, Toivo Glumov, is an investigator in Maxim's Department of Extraordinary

Events *(otdel chrezvychainykh proizshestvii).* He is responsible for discovering the perpetrators of a series of enigmatic, seemingly supernatural occurrences which take place on Earth in the last years of the twenty-third century. Although the extraordinary occurrences, ranging from a streak of suicidal whale beachings to a Hollywood-style "invasion of the slime monster" are logically unrelated, taken together, they seem to imply the active design of a supernatural power. Indeed, the events of the year '99 seem fraught with apocalyptic significance. Toivo is determined to uncover the machinations of an imperialist supercivilization—known hypothetically as the Wanderers—behind the apocalyptic portents. In his relentless pursuit of the cosmic enemy, Toivo stumbles instead upon the mystery of his own double identity: he himself is one of an elect group of superhumans destined to spearhead humanity's evolution into a higher race. Like Oedipus' search for the cause of his people's woes, Toivo's search leads him, finally, back to himself. *The Waves Still the Wind* consists of Maxim Kammerer's memoirs, arranged so as to retrace the mystery of Toivo's fall—paradoxically, ascent—from his own humanity.

Our analysis of *The Beetle in the Anthill* emphasized the role of the prefigurative motif as a familiar point of reference and analogy, which helps the reader to orient among conflicting or ambiguous events presented in the novel. Furthermore, the prefigurative motif in *The Beetle in the Anthill* follows what White has called an "unilinear pattern of development"; that is, the relationship of the actualized plot to the underlying motif is fairly simple and straightforward. In order of their appearance in the story, the legend of the Pied Piper prefigures the characters (jester, children), the imagery (rats, wells in which the adults "drown") and the events (mass disappearance) of Abalkin's planet Hope report. In *The Waves Still the Wind,* this model is distorted. The prefigurative pattern is fragmented, and displaced onto more than one character or situation.

The operative pattern is the life of Jesus, as it is known from the Gospels. The analysis below reconstructs the underlying pattern, and demonstrates how it prefigures the form, although not necessarily the content, of the plot. In other words, although many of the events comprising Toivo's biography are prefigured by the life of Jesus, Toivo's moral and ethical stance is not always "Christ-like." In some instances, allusions to the gospel motif are displaced from Toivo, the central protagonist, to a peripheral character.

The prefigurative motif is alluded to right away, in an introduction which post-dates the main action of the novel. Maxim Kammerer's introduction is couched in secular, pseudo-scientific vocabulary; nevertheless, he implicitly places himself in the role of an apostle, a "witness, participant, and in some sense even an initiator" of the "Big Revelation" *("Bol'shoe Otkrovenie").*

> From the point of view of an unprejudiced reader, especially of the younger generation, this memoir is about the events which brought an end to a whole epoch of humanity's perception of its role in the cosmos. At first, it seemed as though these events opened up completely new perspectives, which had heretofore only been considered theoretically. I was a witness, participant, and in some sense even an initiator of these events . . . which caused such a storm of discussion, misgivings, anxiety, disagreement, indignation, and mainly—enormous surprise—everything which we now call the Big Revelation (8 9).[7]

The central figure of his story, Toivo Glumov, arises in the narrator apostle's memory with many of the features traditionally attributed to Jesus Christ:

> I see his very thin, always serious young face, with long white eyelashes always lowered over the transparent grey eyes. I can hear his seemingly deliberate, slow speech, and once again I can feel a voiceless, helpless, but invincible force emanating from his whole being, like a soundless cry . . . and vice versa, as soon as some association brings Toivo to mind, immediately, as if they had been rudely kicked awake, all the 'evil dogs of memory' spring to life—all the horror of those days, the despair of those days, the helplessness of those days; horror, despair, helplessness, which I had to bear alone, since there was nobody with whom I could share them. (10)

The features of the iconographic Christ—thin, gray-eyed, paradoxically young and serious, helpless and inexorably powerful—seem at first to vindicate the pattern emerging in the prefigurative motif. In the biblical context we have already been alerted to by mention of the Big Revelation, the appearance of a Christ-like central figure in Maxim's memoirs is not incongruous. However, the expected pattern is interrupted in midparagraph, and a piece of the prefigurative motif is dislocated

onto the narrator himself. The second bundle of features that
belong to the Christ figure—his essential aloneness, and despair
(in Gethsemane)—are, on the other hand, claimed for the narrator himself. The passage is a typical example of a device the
Strugatskys will use throughout the novel: fragmentation and
(re)combination of the prefigurative motif. For instance, in the
following scene, Toivo is confronted by one of his colleagues
and the following exchange takes place. It is not necessary to
know the context in which the dialog takes place in order to
recognize a piece of the prefigurative pattern.

> "No," he [Grisha] said. "I just can't do it, I'm not like you. I can't do it.
> This is too serious. Everything in me objects. This isn't a private mat-
> ter, you know: 'I believe, and the rest of you can do what you like.'
> For if I believed, that would mean throwing away everything else, sacri-
> ficing everything that I have and rejecting the rest . . . it would mean
> shaving my head and taking the vows, for Heaven's sake! But our life is
> multifaceted! How can you just peg it into a single thing. . . .
> Although, of course, sometimes I feel frightened and ashamed, and
> then I look at you with delight and admiration. . . . Sometimes, though,
> like right now, just the sight of you makes me furious—your self-torture,
> your fanaticism, your heroic asceticism! It makes me want to joke, to
> make fun of you, and to make light of everything which you are trying
> to dump on us..."
> "Listen, said Toivo, "what do you want from me, anyway?"
> Grisha was silent.
> "Really," he said at last. "What do I want from you? I don't know."
> "Ah, but I know. You want everything to be good and to get better
> every day."
> "O!" Grisha raised his finger. (129 130)

The identification of Toivo with the prefigurative Christ is
intensified here. Following Toivo's example means "sacrificing
everything," and "shaving one's head" (metaphorically: joining
the holy orders). Grisha contemplates Toivo/Christ with
"delight and awe," but feels "ashamed and afraid" in the face of
his example. An element of unorthodox, but very modern
ambiguity enters in at this point—Grisha also feels resentment
and disgust at Toivo's martyrdom. Finally, in a single iconographic gesture, which is both symbolic, and a parodic dis-
placement of that symbol (onto the disciple, Grisha) Christ
raises his finger to admonish and teach: "you want everything
to be good and better every day." Here the biblical prefigura-

tion confronts another motif, which paraphrases the Marxist-Leninist conception of history's linear progress: "the good gets better every day." The fact that Toivo has been reading a book with the title *Vertical Progress* when Grisha walks in is now doubly significant. Toivo's question, and Grisha's honest answer—he doesn't know what he wants from a savior—are connected to the apocalyptic theme in the novel *via* the allusion to linear (vertical) progress: a society which "doesn't know what it wants," except that "the good get better every day," is particularly vulnerable to an exchange of one teleological ideology for another. Thus, the Strugatskys seem to imply, in the twentieth century religion has largely been replaced by communism, or fascism, or an arrogant belief in the omnipotence of science, with a concomitant tendency to replace discredited secular belief systems with a new form of religious fundamentalism.[8]

If, as suggested by the above two examples, the life of Toivo Glumov is prefigured by the life of Jesus as it is known from the most familiar source—the Gospels—then the pattern of events one might expect to find in the novel should include: "baptism, (no childhood, no human father-figure), temptation, gathering of disciples, performing of various miracles, proclaiming a new way of life, a last supper, lonely agony, betrayal, trial, and crucifixion."[9] Since Toivo's life is presented entirely through a selection of documents offered by the narrator, what is surprising is not so much the absence of one or two of the "prefigured" events, as the fact that nearly all of them are present in some form.

Baptism
This point is left out. There is no mention of a baptism.

No childhood, no human father-figure
Nothing is revealed about Toivo's childhood. He appears on the scene as a thirty-year-old man. Fictional transfigurations of Christ usually depict a man of about thirty years, in accordance with what we know of the historical Jesus. According to the chronology of the Strugatskys' future history, Toivo, who is about eleven years old in '78 (in *The Beetle in the Anthill*) is

exactly thirty years old in '99, when the action of *The Waves Still the Wind* takes place. He is not in contact with his father.

The Temptation
The temptation in the wilderness is depicted as one of the mysterious incidents alerting the Committee on Control to the supposed activity of the Wanderers:

> The Committee on Control was notified of an incident on Tissa (not the river Tisa, but on the planet Tissa near Star EN 63061). The report described the incident as a case of sudden madness on the part of all three members of a research party [who] suddenly imagined that their connection with the central base had been lost; indeed, that all communications had been lost, except for with the orbiting mother-ship. Meanwhile, the mother-ship was sending nothing but a news brief to the effect that Earth had been destroyed in some sort of cataclysm, and the population of the entire Periphery had died out due to some sort of unexplained epidemic. . . .
>
> It appears that two members of the party tried to commit suicide, and in the end disappeared into the desert—in despair over the complete lack of hope for future existence. The party's captain . . . forced himself to live as if humanity hadn't actually perished, but he had simply had an accident and been cut off from his native planet forever. Later he recalled that on the fourteenth day of his crazed existence, a figure in white appeared to him and announced that he had successfully passed the first round of trials, and that he would be accepted as a candidate into the society of the Wanderers. (11 12)

Here only the form of the temptation in the wilderness ("desert"), lasting forty ("fourteen") days and ending with the arrival of an angel ("dressed in white") is anticipated by the patterning motif; the spiritual content of the biblical scene is irrelevant. The captain is not a divine figure, nor are the Wanderers necessarily the devil. In this small scene, the plot and imagery anticipated by the prefigurative motif interact with other layers of the text to reinforce the novel's apocalyptic theme (the contents of the "news brief").

Jesus gathers disciples
In the description of Toivo's "gathering of disciples," the Christian motif is simply inverted—Toivo gathers disciples through the intensity of his hate, rather than love. In this he is comparable to another modern literary figure, the Mexican Rivera in

Jack London's story. The following passage provides both the prefigurative and the intertextual allusion:

> It was amazing the way my incumbent staff—Grisha Serosovin, Sandro Mtbevari, Andryusha Kikin, and others—pulled themselves together around him [Toivo]; they stopped lazing around and became less ironic and more efficient. It's not as though they were following his example; there could be no question of that, as he was simply too young and too green for them, but still, it was as if he had infected them with his seriousness, his concentration on the matter at hand, and more than anything, I think they were astonished by the intensity of his hatred towards the object of our research [i.e., the Wanderers], a hatred which was palpable in him, but totally lacking in others. Once I coincidentally mentioned the swarthy boy Rivera to Grisha Serosovin, and not long thereafter discovered that all of my staff had unearthed and reread that story by Jack London. (28 29)

Jesus performs miracles

The "performing of miracles" prefigured in the biblical motif is realized paradoxically by Toivo's fanatical persecution of those he suspects of performing miracles. Every miraculous occurrence is interpreted by Toivo as further evidence of the supercivilization's active and by definition hostile intervention in the course of humanity's development.

Jesus proclaims a new way of life

The historical Jesus' proclamation of a new, Christian world view occurred in a time of spiritual and political turmoil, as old belief systems were broken down and replaced by new ones. The rise of Christianity, like the rise of Islam, was accompanied by a general upsurge in mystical cult activity and the appearance of false prophets. Much of the plot material in *The Waves Still the Wind* is motivated by this formal prefiguration. The era of the "Big Revelation," the subject matter of Maxim Kammerer's memoirs, was characterized by

> the appearance of mass phobias, new messianic movements, people with extraordinary capabilities, as well as the sudden and inexplicable disappearance, as if by magic, of certain people, and the development of new talents in some people, etc. (22)

The proclamation of a "new way of life" is displaced from the figure of Toivo onto a document known as "Bromberg's Memorandum." The Christian ideal of a new, selfless society based on love and spiritual integrity is radically secularized and outfitted with pretensions to scientific veracity.

> Any intelligent form of life . . . in the first phase of its evolution must pass through the stage of maximum discord (savagery, mutual hostilities, deficient emotional life, mistrust) to a condition of maximum concord with the integrity of the individual retained (friendliness, high culture of mutual interaction, altruism, disdain for worldly goods). This process is governed by biological, bio-social, and specifically social laws. (18)

Bromberg's memorandum on the "Monocosm" sets up an opposition between the esoteric, Eastern-influenced ideal of "inner tranquillity, focus within the self, the physical world becomes irrelevant, . . ." and the exoteric, Western-oriented ideal characterized by the "romantic trills of the theory of vertical progress" (18). Bromberg proposes a synthetic metaphysics which leads onto "the path of the Monocosm." The easy interchangeability of mystical and secular doctrines proclaiming a new life is underscored by Bromberg's use of quasi-scientific rhetoric to represent archetypical religious images of Paradise:

> The Synthesis of Reasons . . . leads to the reduction of suffering to a minimum and the increase of joy to a maximum. The concept of "home" expands to include the whole universe. Man develops a new type of metabolism, and as a result life and health become almost eternal. The age of the individual becomes commensurate with the age of the cosmos—without any side-effects of accumulated psychic exhaustion. An individual of the Monocosm does not have need of creators. He himself is his own creator and consumer of culture. . . . Each new individual [of the Monocosm] is born out of a process of synthetic art: he is created by the Monocosm's physiologists, geneticists, engineers, psychologists, aestheticians, pedagogues, and philosophers. (19)

Bromberg's thesis, with its bureaucratic definition of heaven ("reduction of suffering to a minimum") and scientific explanation of how man becomes an angel ("a new type of metabolism") is more than just tongue-in-cheek science fiction. The treatise on the "Synthesis of Reasons" echoes in form and content to the "Synthesis of two kinds of Reason" (*Sintez dvukh razumov*) proposed by the philosopher Nikolai Fyodorov. The influence of Fyodorov on the Strugatskys' writing will be examined in more detail in chapter 4.

The Last Supper

Allusions to the Last Supper are few, and could be considered random detail without prefigurative significance, if they were not located precisely at a turning point in Toivo's career. The context in which the allusions occur is more telling than their frequency. Leading directly up to the last supper scene is Toivo's exchange with Grisha (presented above), the most explicit comparison of Toivo to the figure of Jesus in the novel. Several details of the exchange emphasize Toivo's essential aloneness and foreshadow his complete separation from humanity.

The last supper scene, the only domestic scene in the novel, is immediately preceded by Toivo's wife's description of her troubles at the culinary institute were she works. She complains that the starter (for bread) which they import from Pandora has gone too far and become bitter, thus jeopardizing the further production of a certain kind of leavened cakes which are famous "all over our planet." Her tirade is a good example of the text's multiple layers. Underneath the cliches of science fiction (synthesized food, inter-planetary distribution), the reader clearly hears the colloquial intonational patterns of a contemporary, frustrated urban Soviet working woman. Within the context of "The Last Supper," the allusion to over-leavened bread would seem to be a hint of humorous blasphemy.

The scene is endowed with apocalyptic significance by a portentous, overly dramatic sunset: "They dined in the (living) room, made crimson by the sunset" (131). This "Last Supper" is Toivo's last supper with his wife Asya. She then leaves for a three month business trip, and by the time she returns the "betrayal" (below) has taken place. The biblical imagery in this scene is not from the iconographic Last Supper—Christ with the twelve disciples seated around a table—but from the story of Martha and Mary in the Gospel of Luke (10:38 42). The image of Mary seated at Jesus' feet, listening to his teaching while Martha serves, is somewhat reversed: Toivo is positioned at Asya's feet while he delivers his "sermon" on the relativity of

good and evil. Asya does not bring in supper until Toivo is fin-
ished talking. Then, as Toivo and Asya are eating supper, a
beautiful butterfly flies into the room. They decide to name her
"Martha." The pattern prefigured by the biblical motif is completed.

Christ is betrayed

The "ludens" are a select group of people who have evolved in a
qualitative leap beyond the rest of mankind. A so-called "third
impulse system" renders the ludens psychologically, physiologi-
cally, and intellectually far more advanced than ordinary *homo
sapiens*. The heretofore dormant third impulse system which
determines Toivo's surprise identity as a luden is, quite literally,
the cross (a Latin-script capital T) which he bears:

> Kammerer: [to Toivo] . . . the machine scans a person's mentogram for
> the so-called T-tooth, otherwise known as "Logovenko's impulse." If
> the person has a latent third impulse system which can be initiated, the
> thrice-cursed T-tooth shows up in his mentogram. Well, you show that
> tooth. (201)

The revelation of Toivo's extra-human identity is tantamount
to the "Big Revelation" mentioned in the narrator's introduction. The scientifically verifiable existence of the ludens and
their extraordinary powers (which to an ordinary human seem
like miracles) obviates the need for a hypothetical supercivilization. There is no longer a need to posit the existence of the
Wanderers; in other words, the source of the extraordinary
multi-horned beast and other trials inflicted upon humanity has
not been an alien supercivilization from the other side of the
cosmos. Rather, the apocalyptic signs have been the work of an
internal, alternative, profound Otherness which has evolved
within the bounds of humanity. Thus, the central plot-forming
question, around which the entire future history cycle has
revolved, is laid open to ridicule. In *The Waves Still the Wind*,
Leonid Gorbovsky himself, the patriarch of the future history
cycle, rises from his deathbed (he is now over two hundred and
fifty years old) to ridicule the whole theory of the "Wanderers,"
and, by meta-literary implication, to ridicule a superficial reading of the novel's deceptively popular form:

You're grown-ups, after all, not schoolchildren, not under-grad-
uates. . . . Really, aren't you ashamed of yourselves? This is why I dis-
like all these discussions about the Wanderers, and always have disliked
them! They always lead to precisely this kind of terrified gibberish with
a detective story plot! (181)

The act of betrayal is fragmented across many different layers
of the text, but its significance is assured by its location in the
novel's development. The cluster of perceived and actual
"betrayals" all occur in the scene following Toivo's last supper,
and preceding his departure from earth into outer space
—metaphorically, his ascent to Heaven.

Maxim Kammerer takes the news that Toivo is more than
human as a "betrayal" and as "the loss of a son." He tries to
talk Toivo into becoming a double agent and informing to
humanity on the activities of his own kind. Here the motif of
betrayal prefigured by the biblical pattern is juxtaposed onto a
series of allusions to betrayal in its specific, twentieth-century
Soviet context. For instance, Toivo Glumov, still innocent of
his identity, is allowed to listen to a recorded conversation in
which Earth's foremost representative of the ludens explains
the group's origin and present activities. There are considerable gaps in the recording. However, the authors assume that
readers and survivors of Solzhenitsyn's *The First Circle* will
understand what/who lies behind "the strange manner of
negotiating":

Glumov: So what was in the gaps?
Kammerer: No one knows.
Glumov: What do you mean no one knows?
Kammerer: Just that. Komov and Gorbovsky don't remember what
was in the gaps. They didn't notice any gaps. And it's impossible to
restore the recording. It's not simply erased, it's destroyed. On the
parts of the grid where the gaps are, the molecular structure is
destroyed.
Glumov: A strange manner of negotiating.
Kammerer: We'll have to get used to it. (197)

Toivo's hatred for the Wanderers, now transferred to the
more immediate and concrete target of the ludens, evokes a
new subtext—"the Jewish question."

> Glumov: The point of the matter is that humanity should not be the
> incubator for non-humans, not to mention a testing ground for their
> accursed experiments! . . . You shouldn't have initiated Komov and
> Gorbovsky [members of the World Council] into this matter. You put
> them in a sticky position. This matter is completely within the compe-
> tence of our Committee on Control. I think it is still not too late. Let
> us take this sin upon our souls.
> Kammerer: Listen, where do you get off with this xenophobia? We're
> not talking about the Wanderers, or the Progressors, whom you
> hate . . .
> Glumov: I have a feeling that [the ludens] are even worse than Pro-
> gressors. They are traitors. They are parasites. They are like those
> wasps who lay their eggs in caterpillars' nests. . . . (198)

The hazy allusion to Nazi experiments, to the failure of
international alliances to "contain" fascism in time, and to anti-
Semitic attitudes are reinforced by Toivo's out-of-character
resort to religious terminology: "we must take this sin upon
our souls." On the other hand, there is no one-to-one corre-
spondence between the configuration of the fictional plot and
characters, and the configuration of the sociopolitical events
they allude to. In the passage above, Toivo Glumov—himself
now a luden!—accuses the ludens of using humans as a testing
ground for "accursed (read Nazi) experiments," while simultaneously using the vocabulary of Soviet anti-Semitic propaganda
against them ("wasps who lay their eggs . . .").

Toivo refuses Maxim's offer to work as a double-agent
because he is afraid that as soon as he activates the third
impulse system in order to disguise himself in the ranks of the
enemy, he will lose all traces of his humanity:

> Turning into a luden would be death for me. It would be much worse
> than death, though, because for those who love me, I would still be
> alive, but unrecognizably disgusting. A stuck-up, conceited, arrogant
> type. On top of it, probably, eternal. (207)

It is hard not to add the word "Jew" to the epithet "eternal"
(vechnyi) which is the Russian name for "The Wandering Jew."
Maxim tries to calm Toivo with the words "Nothing terrible has
happened yet. Why are you screaming like that, as if 'smirking,
they approached with knives'? The intertextual allusion is to
Heinrich Heine's *Disputation* (1851), and the verse in full reads
"smirking/ the Jews approached with knives/ to begin the cir-
cumcision. . . ."

Resurrection

The Waves Still the Wind includes the final formal piece of the prefigurative pattern we have been following, i.e., the Resurrection. Toivo joins the minority ranks of the ludens after all, and literally begins a new life beyond Earth, since most ludens prefer to live in outer space. Allusions scattered throughout the novel which link a rise in Russian Nationalism (and anti-Semitism) to apocalyptic fervor become part of an explicit motif by the end of the novel. The elements of the plot and imagery anticipated by the prefigurative motif, such as the sign of the cross, betrayal, and the ascent to outer space (heaven), are fragmented and superimposed onto the pattern of allusions which refers the reader to the dilemma faced by Soviet Jews who consider emigrating. Therefore, although it was tempting for the critic Kaganskaia to read the text as an entirely allegorical cipher for the Strugatskys' attitude toward Soviet anti-Semitism and the question of Jewish emigration, it would seem that the "Jewish question" represents only one facet of the apocalyptic theme which reaches its crescendo in the final part of the future history trilogy. An examination of the topography of the Apocalypse in *The Waves Still the Wind* confirms this interpretation.

The Apocalyptic Beast

The frame story of *The Waves Still the Wind* seems to be prefigured by the canonical plot of Christ's life. Because the prefiguration is displaced and/or incomplete, it suggests that the fact of Christ alone is important and relevant, although the events as well as the morality of the Gospels may not be. Specifically, the presence of a Christ-figure in a society which is braced for cataclysmic change is the object of the Strugatskys' careful, somewhat ambivalent treatment. Within the frame plot, the authors placed a story-within-the-story. The imbedded story describes Toivo's on-location investigation of an incident at the resort village of Malaya Pesha. After all, as we know from Maxim's framing narration, Toivo as a young man was engaged in investigating "extraordinary occurrences." In this particular case, in May, '99, the summer occupants of the dacha settlement Malaya Pesha fled in a panic when they were invaded by a multi-headed, multi-horned beast of unknown origins.

This is how Maxim introduces his retrospective account of the event and the subsequent investigation:

> It's easy to see that the following reconstruction . . . contains not only completely verifiable facts, but also a fair share of descriptions, metaphors, epithets, dialogs, and other elements of fictional literature.
>
> This is my first attempt at literary reconstruction. I have tried my best. My task has been somewhat complicated by the fact that I had never been to Malaya Pesha way back then, when my story takes place; however, I have at my disposal an adequate collection of video tapes. . . . So I can vouch for the accuracy of my topographical descriptions, at least. I also think it is possible to vouch for the accuracy of the dialogs. (76)

As one might expect, the narrator's caveat is misleading. The topography of Malaya Pesha is not reconstructed from any conceivable "videos," but from an eclectic variety of fictional landscapes which already exist as artifacts of Western culture. The pattern of intertextual allusion forms gradually, in counterplay with superficial motivations for the plot. As sources of Maxim's topographical detail we can count

- the landscape paintings of Levitan;
- the biblical Revelation of Saint John;
- Kipling's prose fiction;
- Aleksei Tolstoy's Russian adaptation of *Pinocchio*;
- Ian Fleming's spy novels.

Since in his "reconstructed story" the narrator intends to persuade his audience with feelings, rather than facts, Maxim allows himself a detailed description of the landscape and general atmosphere in which Toivo's investigation took place.

> From above, the village of Malaya Pesha looked just as such a village should look around three o'clock in the morning. Sleepy. Peaceful. Empty. About ten differently colored roofs in a half-circle, a square overgrown with grass, and a yellow club pavilion by the cliff overlooking the river. The river seemed still, very cold and uninviting, with clumps of whitish fog hanging over the reeds on the other side.
>
> The cottages at Malaya Pesha were ancient constructions from the last century: utilitarian architecture in the undecorated organic style—but with the poisonously bright colors of old. Each cottage was thickly surrounded by black currant bushes, lilacs, and polar strawberries. Immediately behind the half-circle of houses, the forest began—the

yellow trunks of gigantic pine trees, the crowns of coniferous trees grey-green in the fog, and above them all—the sun's purple disk, already quiet high in the northeastern sky. (64-5)

The first requirement of the detective is that he should, while on the job, take careful note of every clue provided by the scene of the crime or unusual occurrence. Accordingly, in Maxim's reconstruction, Toivo's perception of interior and exterior landscapes does not reveal anything about the landscape as such; rather, it depicts the landscape as a record of the incident being investigated.

> There were a lot of tracks: the bushes were crushed and broken, the flower bed was ruined, and the grass under the railings looked as if horses had rolled on it. If there had been any animals here, they had been clumsy, cumbersome animals, and they hadn't crept up to the house, but barged towards it headlong. They had come from the square, straight through the bushes, and then into the house through the open windows. . . .
>
> Toivo crossed the veranda and pushed open the door into the house. Inside there were no signs of disorder. At least, not of the sort that would have been caused by heavy and unwieldy carcasses.
>
> A sofa. Three chairs. No table in sight—it must be built in. Only one control panel—in the arm of the owner's armchair. . . . On the front wall—a Levitan landscape, an ancient chromophoto likeness touchingly marked with a tiny triangle in the lower left corner, so that, God forbid, some expert wouldn't be fooled into taking it for an original. (74)

The landscape of Malaya Pesha provides clues to the science fiction plot as well as to the underlying philosophical plot of the novel. The Strugatskys use the formulaic conventions of the detective story not only to build a suspenseful plot, but also to more firmly anchor the "fantastic" story to a contemporary political and philosophical agenda. In order to understand how this is done, it is necessary to recall that setting and milieu in the detective story have a pragmatic, rather than semantic function.[10] In other words, setting and milieu in the detective story are not depicted in the same sense as they are in other genres. The scene of a crime or mysterious occurrence is not a romantic or realistic painting of nature or of a drawing room; rather, it is a model of a locality which has retained the imprint of some human activity. Human activity is objectified (*versachlicht*)

in the topography of the crime novel.[11] Thus, in the passage
above, the interior and exterior landscape of Malaya Pesha
clearly records a hasty departure from the veranda, evidence of
an enormous beast coming through the garden, and a puzzling
lack of disorder within the house the beast supposedly entered.

On the other hand, futuristic gadgetry (armchair control
panel, "chromophoto likeness," etc.) and internationalized lexi-
con notwithstanding, the landscape of Malaya Pesha also
denotes a contemporary socio-cultural milieu which is important to the underlying philosophical plot. The description of the
dacha resort and the surrounding landscape oozes with nostal-
gia for the unspoiled North Russian countryside. Only the
birches are missing; otherwise, the misty waterways and towering pine trees are almost a caricature of Levitan's melancholy
landscape paintings, one of which duly appears a few pages
later (quoted above). This landscape, with its parodic overtones, does not reflect a natural setting; it describes a milieu in
which Russian nationalist sentiments play a significant role.
What this role is becomes clearer as the apocalyptic subtext
develops.

A further requirement for the plausible depiction of Toivo's
investigative techniques is that his habit of noting times, dates,
and numbers with excruciating accuracy must be replicated.
Nevertheless, the density of seemingly extraneous statistical
detail in the story disrupts the flow of the narrative. One
begins to wonder whether the aesthetic price paid for remaining faithful to the task of depicting a dry, boring, fanatical
investigator at work is worth it. Not surprisingly, the aesthetic
"loss" turns out to be an informational "gain" (the cognitive
gain may then become, after all, an aesthetic gain).

The second part of the reconstructed story begins in chapter
6 of the novel. It opens with an excess of numbers:

> Chapter 6
> Malaya Pesha. 6. May '99 6 a.m.
> On May 5, around 11 pm, in the resort village of Malaya Pesha
> (thirteen cottages, eighteen residents), a panic broke out. (79)

The coincidence of three sixes which arises in the combination of the chapter number (belonging to the novel's outer

frame), the date, and the time (belonging to the inner frame) becomes significant in light of the "excessive" statistical detail offered in parentheses: (thirteen cottages, eighteen residents). Chapter 13, line 18, of Revelation reads:

> This calls for wisdom: let him who has understanding reckon the number of the beast, for it is a human number, its number is 666.

The beast referred to in Rev. 13:18 soon appears in the reconstructed topography of chapter 6, written at 6 a.m. on May 6th:

> a panic broke out. The cause of the panic was the arrival of a certain (unknown) number of quasi-biological creatures of extremely repulsive, and even rather frightening appearance. (79)

The beast which invades the resort village is variously described as having many eyes and many horns. Therefore, "the beast" is always referred to in the plural. As in the biblical Apocalypse, the appearance of the beast(s) in Malaya Pesha divides the population into two groups: the select, and the damned. In fact, in the perception of the resort community, it is two different beasts: a few people see in it part of God's host, one of the four living creatures "full of eyes before and behind" described in Rev. 4:6; the majority see one of Satan's agents, who is frightening in appearance and has many horns, like the beast from the sea described in Rev. 13:1-10. The latter react to the beast's presence in sheer, apocalyptic terror:

> "You say they [the beast] can 'frighten'. . . [a witness] said through gritted teeth, without raising his eyes. "'Frighten' would be nice! You know, they can scare you to death!" (76)

Only a child and an old lady recognize not a beast, but one of God's "living creatures" mentioned in Revelation, chapter 4. The Strugatskys avoid cliche, however, by emphasizing neither the innocence of childhood nor the wisdom of old age *per se* as saving qualities. Instead, what the "saved" have in common is an elusive otherworldliness, which can be traced to their literary origins within a different text.

A small, tanned boy shows up in the deserted, apocalyptic village as the investigators are eating lunch. He tells the investigators that his name is Kir, and he has returned to the family's dacha to pick up his galleyship. The boy's model galleyship becomes a leitmotif which accompanies him through the rest of the chapter. Just as Kir's galleyship can be seen as a toy model of the galleyship in Kipling's "The Greatest Story in the World," everything else in the Northern Russian dacha resort, seen through Kir's eyes, becomes a kind of toy model of Kipling's world. As the Strugatskys' emissary from another fictional world, the character Kir (Kipling's "Kim") embodies the sensibilities of that world. For him, multi-horned beast(s) are

> nice, funny . . . They re soft, and silky, like mongooses [*sic*], except without fur . . . And so what if they're big. Tigers are big, too, and am I supposed to be afraid of tigers or something? They smell good, also! They smell like berries! I think they probably feed on berries . . . We should domesticate them, what's the use of running away from them? (85)

One other inhabitant of Malaya Pesha recognizes, like Kir, a Lamb instead of a Beast. However, the old woman's aura of otherworldliness derives from a different literary tradition. Whereas Kir's arrival on the scene is whimsically and comically inopportune—the inspector is caught in mid-swallow, holding a half-eaten cold sandwich—the old woman's arrival aspires to something more like the materialization of Woland at Patriarchs' Pond:[12]

> It was already becoming noticeably hotter in the sun, and the sky was cloudless. Blue dragonflies flickered above the lush grass on the square. Then, appearing through their metallic flickering like a bizarre daylight apparition, a majestic old lady floated towards the pavilion with an expression of infinite aloofness on her narrow brown face.
> Holding up (devilishly elegantly) the hem of her snowy-white dress, she seemed not to even touch the grass as she glided up to Toivo and stopped. . . . .
> "You may call me Albina," she said graciously in a pleasant baritone. (87)

Toivo's interview with the otherworldly Albina is, paradoxically, precisely that point in the story which intersects with the plane of contemporary socio-political commentary. The old woman recognizes in the villagers' terror nothing but the abject reflection of their own spiritual poverty:

"How could it happen that in our times, at the end of our century, right here on Earth a living creature, beseeching people for help and mercy, not only received neither help nor mercy, but was actually made the object of baiting, threats, and even active physical violence of the most barbaric nature. I don't mean to mention any names, but they beat them with rakes, they yelled at them like madmen, they even tried to crush them with their gliders. I would never have believed it, if I hadn't seen it with my own eyes. Are you familiar with the concept of savagery? Well, this was savagery! I am ashamed.

. . . Well, then, be so kind as to explain! Understand me correctly, the issue is not whether to apply some sort of sanctions. But we must be able to understand how it is possible for people who still yesterday were civilized, cultured, wonderful people, . . . how today they suddenly lose their human face! Do you know what differentiates Man from all the other animals?"

"Uh . . . reason?" Toivo suggested.

"No, my dear! Mercy! Mer - cy!" (87 88)

Albina's answer reinforces the biblical subtext, and adds an ironic twist to the apocalyptic motif. In her version of the Malaya Pesha incident, it was not people who called upon God for charity and mercy from the Beast's scourges; but vice versa, the Beast, according to Albina, called upon humans for charity and mercy—only to be rebuked and reviled by the resort's inhabitants. Thus, Albina's reference to "the end of our age" applies equally to chronological time and to Christian eschatology. When there is no longer charity or mercy in human hearts, it signals the end of our age, and the advent of the antichrist. Underneath the comedy of manners which characterizes Toivo's meeting with the formidable old lady is the Strugatskys' bitter reminder to the Russian reader that the Russian word for mercy, *miloserdie*, was absent for decades from Soviet editions of the standard Russian Language Dictionary.

As Toivo's investigation continues, the village's frightened vacationers return, one by one, to their dachas. The rest of the story takes on a carnivalesque tone, as each inhabitant of Malaya Pesha seems to spring fully grown out of another text.

The inhabitants of cottage No. 10 turn out to be one Oleg Olegovich Pankratov, and his wife Zosya. The physical description of Oleg is that of one of the *bogatyrs* in Vasnetsov's famous romantic painting of the "Three Bogatyrs." Toivo finds out that Oleg's reaction to the beast was "disgust" rather than fear, and with hands "like shovels" he pushed its intruding jellyish carcasses back out of his window and into the yard. If Oleg is a caricature of the Russian folk hero, his wife is presented as a caricature of the refined artist-intellectual. Zosya evokes an aesthetic theory in order to put distance between herself and her intuitive horror at the sight of the beast:

> those monsters . . . were so frightful and repulsive, that in their own way they were perfect. The perfection of sheer ugliness. The aesthetic clash of ideal ugliness with ideal beauty. Someone once said that ideal ugliness should actually evoke the same aesthetic response as ideal beauty. Until last night, she [Zosya] had always considered that a paradox. But it's not a paradox! Or has she simply become such a perverted individual? (97)

In the initial stages of Toivo's investigation, a man by the name of Alexander Jonathan (Russian version of this name would be Ioann, an anagram of Ian) Fleming emerges as the prime suspect capable of unleashing the incredible multi-beast upon the resort village. Fleming is the operator of a bio-engineering laboratory not far from Malaya Pesha. Toivo figures that the beast could have been an escaped creation of Fleming's bio-genetic technology. The occupants of cottage No. 7 return with a bag of "craycrabs" (a bio-hybrid from Fleming's laboratory), a culinary delight which they insist is "only of the freshest quality." (In Bulgakov's *The Master and Margarita*, a famous passage describes the sturgeon with the same words.) The direct allusion to Bulgakov is followed by a playful evocation of Aleksei Nikolaevich Tolstoy, author of *The Golden Key*, a Russian version of the Pinocchio story. One of the two vacationing gourmets is named Lev Nikolaevich Tolstov, an approximation of the name of Aleksei Tolstoy's famous relative. True to the spirit of carnival, he is described as a buffoonish figure out of *The Golden Key*, like

> kind old Duremar right out of Auntie Tortilla's pond—an elongated, long-haired, long-nosed, emaciated figure wearing a nondescript cape, and plastered with drying slime *(Waves, 80)*.

In another carnivalesque twist, this L. N. Tolstov works at the local branch of Fleming's laboratory; therefore, he is in a position to lambast the theory that the beast which visited Malaya Pesha could have been artificially constructed. His tirade doubles as motivation for the surface plot (clearly, Toivo must now abandon this easy explanation of the beast's origin) and as a meta-literary comment on the lack of credible science in most science fiction.

> Do you have any idea of what you are talking about? Do you have even the slightest conception of the subject? Have you ever even seen an artificial organism? Oh, in a newsreel flick? Well look, there is not and cannot be an artificial organism capable of crawling into people's bed-room windows. . . . Have you tried to consider how much energy would be necessary for an embryophor to develop to such a mass even over the course of a whole hour? (82)

The function of the eclectic intertextual allusions is not clear, although the burlesque incongruities in general, and the paro-dic portrait of Tolstoy in particular, suggest a conscious allusion to the work of the Russian absurdist Kharms.[13] At this point, one can draw the preliminary conclusion that the Strugatskys find the style of the Russian absurdists more relevant to the end of our age than the grandiose apocalyptic images of the symbol-ist writers. Still, it is clear that the Revelation of Saint John shapes the setting of Toivo's investigation. Under the guise of science fiction, the imbedded story of Malaya Pesha is a fantas-tic parable about humanity's reaction to the coming of the antichrist.

In the final scene of Maxim's imbedded story, the "Second Coming" is not only thoroughly secularized, it is also devoid of all revolutionary and mystic overtones. Duremar-Tolstov is last seen leaving cottage No. 7 in great haste and much preoccu-pied, pausing to announce in a penetrating falsetto "I will return—soon" ["*Da vernus' ia skoro*"] a parodic echo of the Lord's words in Rev. 22:7 "And behold, I am coming soon" ["*ce, gradu skoro*"]. Duremar-Tolstov's return looks like a film clip from "Miami Vice"—not entirely out of keeping with his inter-textual relationship to Ian Fleming:

> Suddenly a shadow fell over Malaya Pesha, the air was filled with a vel-vety cooing, Basil [an inspector] shot out of the pavilion pulling on his jacket as he ran, but then once again the sun was shining over Malaya Pesha. A ship descended onto the square, majestically, without bending a single blade of grass, all shiny and gold, like a gigantic round loaf of bread, one of the newest, super-modern, 'Puma' class ships. All its

portholes sprung open instantaneously, and long-legged, tanned, busy, shouting men poured out onto the square, dragging with them crates with funnels, hoses with bizarre tips, blitz-contacts which sparkled. . . People were running around and waving their hands, but the person who was running and waving his hands and hauling boxes and pulling hoses most of all was Lev-Duremar Tolstov, still in the clothes which were plastered with green, dried-up slime. (100)

It is hard to take the finale of the Malaya Pesha story seriously. The imbedded story successfully models a situation of crisis with apocalyptic overtones, but it does not offer a way out. Casting the slime-covered Duremar-Tolstov in the role of a Savior is a travesty which debases not so much the content of the apocalyptic parable as its modern style. With the exception of Albina and Kir, the segment of humanity tested fails completely to grasp the implication of the trial inflicted upon it. In *The Waves Still the Wind* the Strugatskys appropriate the genre of apocalyptic writing, but reject the grandiose and revolutionary tone of most of their models.

The False Prophet of Islam

Modern novelists who choose to use the technique of prefiguration as a means of authorial comment usually rely on a fairly straightforward and familiar cultural motif to provide the anticipatory pattern from which the modern text can deviate. Obviously, the more familiar the reader is with the prefigurative motif—whether it derives from religious or classical mythology or the "new mythologies" of pop culture—the greater its impact on the reader's understanding of the modern text. Of the three prefigurative motifs examined in this chapter, the legend of the Pied Piper is assumed to be universally familiar in European culture; moreover, there is already a precedent for its use as a prefigurative motif in twentieth-century Russian literature, in Tsvetaeva's satirical poem *Krysolov*.[14] Likewise, despite three generations of officially espoused state atheism (and a shortage of Bibles), the Strugatskys might have assumed that some of their readers would recognize the story in the Gospels, or at least its central figure. Nevertheless, in their last novel, *Burdened with Evil, or Forty Years Later*, the Strugatskys apparently set out to consciously reverse what they perceive as a declining awareness of sources. Plot, imagery and characterization in *Burdened with Evil* are largely determined by a web of prefigurative motifs which the authors have spun together into a fantastic tale. In this case, however, most of the prefigurative patterns which would ostensibly govern the reader's understanding of the text are neither familiar nor simple. In an interesting reversal of the didactic function of prefiguration, rather than relying on a well-known motif to function as a substitute for direct authorial comment, the Strugatskys introduce little known or forgotten texts and force the reader to re-discover the source of the literary pattern.

Several of the more esoteric prefigurative texts function only briefly to motivate a single scene or characterization. In the example below, the narrator is a graduate student in a provincial Soviet pedagogical institute in the mid-twenty-first century. He is on a field trip with his teacher (known by his initials, "G.A.") and a fellow pedagogy student. They visit the campsite of a local counter-culture commune, and there they witness two of the cult's members nonchalantly copulating while their leader preaches passivity and apathy towards the establishment world. His description of the scene is directly prefigured by another text, to which he supplies his own reference:

> I was unbearably embarrassed. I averted my gaze and gave up trying to understand them. It was awful to realize that everyone saw what I did, including Misha and G.A. I was also embarrassed for the [commune members], but they didn't seem shocked at all. They just watched the copulating pair with curiosity, and even approval.
>
> "Suddenly a strange staccato was heard in the bushes, a sound I had not ever heard before. It was a series of loud, abrupt O-O-O; the first O was accented, and separated from the following ones by a noticeable pause. The sound was repeated again and again, and within two or three minutes I had discovered its cause: Di Ji was mating with a female."
>
> Question: where does that passage come from? Answer: D. B. Shaller, *Year of the Gorilla* (508).[15]

The allusion to Shaller's study of primate behavior is not isolated or incidental, since it occurs as part of a pattern of allusions developed throughout the novel. The theme of this pattern is the conflict between biological (materialist) and spiritual (idealist) definitions of *homo sapiens*. As such, the novel plays with the similarities and discrepancies between post-modern scientific discourse (the narrator-protagonist is an astro-physicist) and the religious world view of the Christian heresy known as Gnosticism. Fundamental to the system of beliefs espoused by the gnostics is the primacy of transcendental human knowledge (gained through mystical and esoteric revelation) and the inherent evil of all matter.

The gnostic motif established already in the title of the novel is the source of most of the novel's fantastic imagery. Lest the reader miss the importance of the gnostic motif to the metaphysical discussion played out in the novel, the narrator's introduction provides the source of reference.

> I remember that Georgii Anatolevich had told me that the manuscript had been found a few years ago when they tore down the hotel-dormitory of the Steppe Observatory, the oldest scientific institute in our region. The manuscript was inside an old-fashioned paper folder, wrapped in an old-fashioned plastic bag fastened to the folder with two thin black rubber bands. There was no name and no title on the folder, only two large letters written in blue ink: O and 3. At first I thought that these were the figures "zero" and "three." Only many years later did I make the connection between the letters and the epigraph on the folder's inside flap: "the gnostic DEMIURGE is the creative power who makes matter, which is burdened with evil." Then I realized that O3 [cyrillic letters for OZ] is probably an abbreviation for "the burden of evil" or for "[those] burdened with evil" (*otiagoshchennye zlom*)   and the latter is what the unknown author chose to title his manuscript. (Incidently, one could still assume quite justifiably that O3 is not a combination of letters, but of numerals. Then the name of the manuscript is zero-three, which is the telephone number you dial for emergency help—and the title suddenly acquires special, and even ominous meaning. . . .) (486).[16]

The narrator alternates excerpts from his own diary (dated in the mid-twenty-first century) with excerpts from the mysterious manuscript given to him by his teacher. The manuscript itself purports to be the diary of an astronomer who worked at the Steppe Observatory forty years earlier, in the last decade of the twentieth century. The astronomer's diary describes the visitation of a Demiurge and the Wandering Jew to the provincial Soviet town of Tashlinsk. The fictional name can be interpreted as an amalgam of Tashkent and Minsk, i.e., a symbolic microcosm of the Soviet Union, from north to south and east to west. The astronomer's diary belongs to our (the reader's) present time, but is presented as a historical document.

The figure of the Wandering Jew in this novel goes by the name "Agasfer Lukich," a Russianized version of his traditional name, Ahasuerus. His presence is anticipated in one of the two epigraphs to the novel, which reads:

> *Then Simon Peter, having a sword, drew it and struck the high priest's slave and cut off his right ear. The slave's name was Malchus.* The Gospel According to John.

One of the two fundamental motifs which combined to form the Legend of the Wandering Jew is the motif of the violence, or insult, inflicted upon the Savior by an officer of the High Priest (John.18:20 22), whose slave, named Malchus, comes to be identified with the officer. The punishment inflicted upon the one who offended Christ is that he will be doomed to eternal wandering. The motif of eternal wandering was borrowed from the Legend of St. John, according to which John has never died. Since Christ said "If it is my will that he remain until I come, what is that to you?" (John 21:23), legend has it that "the disciple whom Jesus loved" (21:20) did not die at Ephesus, nor in exile on the island of Patmos. Instead, his identity as an awaiter (for the Second Coming) and a wanderer (through history) merges with the Legend of the Wandering Jew.[17]

In his late twentieth-century incarnation on the satirical-fantastic plane of the Strugatskys' text, the Wandering Jew is a buffoonish character who relishes food and drink, not unlike the cat Behemoth in *The Master and Margarita*. During his stay in the town of Tashlinsk, he poses as an insurance agent who has taken a room in the same hotel-dormitory in which the astronomer resides. The stories with which he regales his fellow dormitory residents—and which the astronomer duly records in his diary—are in fact a retelling of the Legend of St. John. That is, Agasfer Lukich's first-person (autobiographical) account of his activities at Ephesus and on the island of Patmos are transformed by the astronomer into recorded speech in the third person.

Agasfer's subsequent peregrinations through history are prefigured by a variety of other texts. Surprisingly, one episode in
Agasfer's life (and in the plot of *Burdened with Evil*) is based on
a scholarly essay first published in 1922 by the distinguished
Russian Orientalist V. V. Bartold.[18]

The story of the "false prophet of Islam" is told in three successive entries of the astronomer's manuscript. At first glance,
the appearance of a seventh-century Arab in the hotel-dormitory, and the ensuing fight to death between the visitor and
Agasfer, seems to carry little more information than the addi-
tion of yet another picaresque episode in the Wandering Jew's
eternal sojourn on earth. In order to better understand the
story of the "false prophet of Islam" and the numerous Russian
calques from Arabic which the Strugatskys incorporated into
this scene, it is helpful to look at the unusual source of the literary prefiguration.

In his essay "Museilima," Bartold reconstructs from scant
available evidence the role of the religious-political leader of
Yemama in the general *ridda*, or "apostasy" (literally, a
"rejection" of Islam), which engulfed the Arabian peninsula
shortly after Muhammad's death. For a period of several years,
until all of Arabia became united in the cause of Islam, several
rival prophets to Muhammad attracted considerable tribal support. Museilima was the most important of the "false
prophets." He seemed to command the loyalty of the sedentary
tribe of the Bani Hanifa, part of a larger confederation opposed
to Muhammad's main constituency. Museilima tried to form an
alliance with a false prophetess named Sajah. One "highly suspect" source depicts the alliance between Museilima and Sajah
as a lewd relationship, their supposed wedding culminating in a
"lustful orgy." This is the version the Strugatskys have chosen
to fictionalize, although Bartold, Eickelman, and "most European sources agree that this account was a later invention
designed to blacken the reputation of the two."[19] All sources
agree that Sajah was absent at the decisive battle of Akraba in
634, when Museilima's troops were defeated and he himself
met his death.

Part of Museilima's great authority, according to Eickelman,
derived from his special use of language:

Unlike ordinary speech, which is in prose, Musaylima's revelations take the form of oaths using unusual words or images, or *sadj'* verse, short sentences in rhythmic prose, with single or more rarely alternating rhyme. . . . Anyone wishing to establish a claim to supernatural communication in seventh-century Arabia was obligated, at least at the beginning of his career, to exhibit the traditionally recognized form of communication with the supernatural. All speech whose origin was attributed to unseen powers, or had something to do with the unseen powers, such as cursing, blessing, divination, incantation, inspiration, and revelation, had to be couched in *sadj'* (Eickelman, 36).

Bartold quotes liberally in Russian translation from the Arabic *sadj'*, or revelatory verse, attributed to Museilima. The Strugatskys have adopted these quotations, word for word, into their own context.

In *Burdened with Evil,* the dormitory in which the Demiurge and the Wandering Jew are staying is visited by Mudzha ibn-Murara, who, according to Bartold, stood at the head of Museilima's minuscule division of troops at the battle at Akraba. All of Museilima's men were killed except Mudzha himself, "which in and of itself bears witness to his readiness to be useful to the Muslim side" (Bartold, 570). In other words, the historical Mudzha ibn-Murara was a traitor to the "false prophet" Museilima, as well as a rather fickle turn-coat in regard to the true prophet Muhammad, whose troops he subsequently deceived as well.

The first section of the Strugatskys' story begins when the astronomer is awakened in the middle of the night by a loud voice asserting that "it is not for the slave to fight, his task is to milk the camels and tie up their udders" *(Burdened,* 610). The voice belongs to a visitor, who addresses his strange statement to Agasfer Lukich. The latter has obviously gotten out of bed in order to bar the visitor's entrance into the Demiurge's reception room. The Wandering Jew's twentieth-century incarnation as a provincial Soviet insurance agent is epitomized by the narrator's observation that

the corner of a black woolen scarf was sticking out from under Agasfer's shirt. He wore this scarf at night as a waistband for protection against the onset of rheumatism. He hadn't even had time to put on his false ear. . . . (610)

Only the mention of his false ear, rather than the false teeth one might expect, serve to remind us that the Wandering Jew is also linked, in some versions of the legend, to the slave Malchus, whose ear was cut off by Simon Peter. He has been wandering through history ever since; therefore, he has no trouble recognizing the visitor from seventh-century Arabia. Far from being perplexed by the visitor's statement, he answers immediately with a quote which is equally enigmatic to the narrator (and reader), but quite meaningful for the visitor:

> "Protect your pastures, give shelter to those who seek it, and drive away the bold." Why don't you say those words to me, Mudzha ibn-Murara?

In what context do we find these exact words in Bartold?

> "Those who have sowed the fields, gathered the crops, hulled the wheat, ground it into flour, baked the bread, cut it into pieces, and eaten the pieces with lard and butter. . . you are better than the nomads and not worse than the city people; protect your pastures, give shelter to those you seek it, and drive away the attackers" (recorded by Bartold, 566).

The Bani-Hanifa tribe which settled in Yemama was essentially an agricultural society, with generally hostile relations toward the surrounding nomadic tribes. Museilima, as religious and political ruler over the Yemamites, offered the above "revelation" in praise of his settled farmers. In the O3 manuscript, the visitor has returned to confront Agasfer-as-Museilima, the false prophet of Islam. The visitor Mudzha ibn-Murara once betrayed Museilima at the battle of Akraba. Now he intends to gain the audience of the Demiurge—for him, the Merciful One, the Islamic Rahman—and beg forgiveness for his sins. The exchange between Museilima-Agasfer and the visitor Mudzha ibn-Murara is presented as a fantastic medley of largely incomprehensible (at first) Islamic oaths, Arabian Night style exoticism, and grotesque violence:

> I swear by the hot samum and by the crazed camel, I will hack off your second ear with my yemenite dagger! (612)

The visitor threatens Agasfer. Agasfer responds by invoking a host of Arabian ghosts and spirits. The narrator comments:

> Someone keep breathing behind my ear. I turned around. Afrits and
> genii all over the place. The whole brigade in full attendance. They
> were all deshabille. . . . (612)

The atmosphere of whimsical, exotic magic, couched in a
mixture of Soviet cliches and gauloiserie, thickens into a darker
mixture of eroticism and passion by the end of the section. The
historical visitor reminds Agasfer, that in another incarnation,
as Museilima, he was betrayed by Sajah, cast here as the femme
fatale.

> "Your Sajah scribbled down that note to you while riding on the
> mighty bough of my man. You know him—Bara ibn-Malik, fiery and
> crazy as a Khavazin colt, fattened on roasted pork, a skilled seducer of
> women, who knows how to get from them anything he needs. And
> what he needed then was for the devil [Agasfer], tormented by lust, to
> abandon Museilima's troops. . . ."
>   Immediately, without pause:
>   "You have allowed yourself the impermissible. . . . "
>   . . . a long, narrow blade flashed for a moment, followed by a
> squashing sound, . . . then there was a croak like a horse's and the
> awful splashing of liquid pouring onto the linoleum. (614 615)

Sections of Bartold's non-fictional essay also anticipate details
of the Strugatskys' setting. For example, in Bartold we find

> [the scholar] Tabari, in his most important, albeit factually unreliable
> essay on the apostasy, quotes from the writings of Sejf the following
> dialog between Museilima and an Arab from a tribe related to the Han-
> ifa. The Arab asked Museilima: "Who comes to you?" Museilima
> answered: "Rahman." "In the light of the day or in darkness?" "In
> darkness." "I testify that you are a liar, and Muhammad said the truth;
> but a liar from the tribe of Rabi'a is still dearer to me than the
> Mudarite who tells the truth" (Bartold, 562).

In the confrontation between Agasfer and his opponent
Mudzha ibn-Murara in *Burdened with Evil,* the content of the
prefigurative text is irrelevant, but the form is adapted for the
authors purposes. The question "in the light of day or in the
dark?" is transformed into an aspect of the Strugatskys' cryptic
setting.   Mudzha ibn-Murara is standing on the threshold
between the dormitory stairwell and the Demiurge's reception
room. The doorway has blurred out of focus to become simply
a triangular aperture dividing the light of the room from the
darkness beyond, where the stairwell used to be. The floor of

the dormitory room is covered with green linoleum (20th-century Russian *byt*), whereas the visitor is standing on a "luxuriously flowered carpet" (seventh-century Arabian realia), the corner of which protrudes across the threshold onto the linoleum. The spatial representation of two temporally distant worlds has a cinematographic quality here. The visitor glances over his shoulder back into the darkness, into historical Arabia, as if listening for the voice of revelation. The play of darkness and light sets the stage for the dialog prefigured by Bartold's essay:

> as if listening for a cue, the visitor [Mudzha ibn-Murara] glanced back over his fat shoulder into the darkness of the triangular aperture. . . .
> "I testify that you are a liar, . . ." the fat man croaked, not having received any support out of the darkness. (611)

I chose to examine this particular instance of the Strugatskys' use of literary prefiguration because it shows the limits to which the device can be used successfully. Although it exhibits the technique of basing a modern text on an anticipatory pattern, it sacrifices much of the meaning the device is meant to provide. Neither Bartold's essay nor its general topic is part of a cultural mythology familiar to most Western or Russian readers. *Burdened with Evil,* according to Boris Strugatsky (in private conversation, 1989), was meant to be "a novel about three Christs." The most familiar and sustained prefigurative motif in *Burdened with Evil* is the life of Christ, which is refracted through the characterization of "G.A.," the Demiurge, and the historical Jesus (as recalled by Agasfer Lukich). However, the novel is equally a novel about false prophets. After two thousand years of Christianity, the humanity depicted in this novel is less prepared than ever for the Second Coming. Each Christ figure in the novel is foiled by false prophets, including Stalin, Hitler, the "punk" leader of the counter-culture commune, and, in the more obscure prefiguration examined above, the false prophet of Islam.

Notes

1. *The Inhabited Island* was translated into English as *Prisoners of Power* (New York: Macmillan, 1977), with an introduction by Theodore Sturgeon. In this novel Maksim (Maxim) Kammerer is introduced as a novice Progressor who lands on a planet which is inhabited by a kind of anti-civilization: a post-holocaust world divided among warring totalitarian regimes. He tries to side with a small population of dissidents and help overthrow the regime. His intentions—and the good guys, bad guys adventure story one has been led to expect—are undermined by political and psychological ambiguities. In subtle ways, the dissidents are as unpleasant and manipulative as the elite which is power. The novel is a classic example of the use of "Aesopian language" and science fiction conventions to circumvent censorship of a blatantly critical model of Soviet political reality. Even so, the Strugatskys were obliged to compromise with the censors and change many aspects of the original version. The full original version will finally be available when the new Tekst edition is published. As an "Aesopian" portrait of the social, political, and psychological tensions within Soviet society on the brink of collapse in the 1970s, the novel traces the contours of glasnost and perestroika before anyone, including the authors, could predict exactly when they would appear on the map.

2. My translations of *The Beetle in the Anthill* and all page citations refer to the edition reprinted in book form along with a few earlier short stories: *Zhuk v muraveinike: rasskazy i povesti* (Riga: Liesma, 1986).

3. Maia Kaganskaia, *"Rokovye Iaitsa,"* *Dvadtsat' Dva*, no. 55 (1987): 173.

4. Walter Mieder, *Tradition and Innovation in Folk Literature* (Hanover, N.H.: University Press of New England, 1987). According to Mieder, the Brothers Grimm compiled their version of the Pied Piper story from several sources already in circulation, but after its publication in 1816, the Grimm version became the primary text against which subsequent adaptations were compared.

5. From *The Complete Works of Robert Browning*, vol. 3 (Athens: University of Ohio Press, 1971).

6. "Was Abalkin's murder justified?" sparked heated debate among Strugatskys fans. In science fiction clubs whole evenings of discussion were devoted (inconclusively) to this topic.

7. *Volni gasiat veter* (The Waves Still the Wind) was published serially in *Znanie-sila*, issues 6-12 (1985) and 1-3 (1986). It was reprinted abroad

and distributed by The Keshet Bookshop (Haifa, Israel). My translations and page numbers refer to the Haifa edition.

8. In the name of Progress, modern societies (both East and West) have sought the path to utopia in scientific and technological "solutions." As a result, the Apocalypse promised by Religion threatens from another side: the danger of a man-made nuclear holocaust or the destruction of the biosphere. The Strugatskys clearly make the connection between the cultural apocalypse and environmental cataclysm. While the present discussion concentrates on the apocalyptic results of instituting Marxist-Leninist notions of "scientific" historical and economic development, the concomitant destruction of the environment for ideological and political reasons is always made implicit. As early as *Far Rainbow* (1962), technology unleashes environmental disaster. *Roadside Picnic* (1972) proved to be a prescient model of how the military-industrial complex (capitalist or socialist) cannot limit an out-of-control technology, but will instead try to prosper from it, regardless of the risk to human populations.

9. Theodore Ziolkowski, *Fictional Transfigurations of Jesus* (Princeton, N.J.: Princeton University Press, 1972), 10. He adds: "The resurrection intrudes into the realm of Christian faith; the historical Jesus was crucified, but only the kerygmatic Christ of faith was resurrected."

10. I. I. Revzin, "Notes on the Semiotic Analysis of Detective Novels: With Examples from the Novels of Agatha Christie," reprinted and translated in *New Literary History* (Vol. 9, No. 2, Winter 1978), 385-8. Originally published in "Programma i tezisy dokladov v letnei shkole po vtorichnym modeliruiushchim sistemam" (Tartu, 1964). Revzin formulates his conclusion from a semiotic analysis of detective story conventions: "The detective novel is a construction in which no reality stands behind the sign, [since in it] the sign does not have a semantic function linked with sense, but only syntactic and pragmatic functions."

11. Heissenbuttel, "Spielregeln des Kriminalromans," *Über Literatur* (Olten: Walter Verlag, 1966), 96-112.

12. Readers familiar with the first chapter of Bulgakov's *The Master and Margarita* will recognize the similarities between Albina's materialization in the midday heat, her devilishly elegant (*"diavol'ski elegantno"*) style and baritone voice, and the Devil's appearance to the two writers at the Patriarchs' Ponds.

13. Daniil Kharms (1905-1941), along with Alexander Vvedensky, formed the nucleus of a short-lived "absurdist" movement in Russian letters in the late 1920s. Both writers died in prison in 1941, and *samizdat* copies of their works began to circulate again only after two decades. A well-known parody of Leo Nikolaevich Tolstoy by Kharms existed in *samizdat*.

14. For a full treatment of the Pied Piper motif in Tsvetaeva's poem, see Günther Wytrzen, *"Eine russische dichterische Gestaltung der Sage vom Hamelner Rattenfänger,"* (Verlag der Österreichischen Akademie der Wissenschaften, Band 395, Vienna, 1981).

15. *Otiagoshchennye zlom, ili sorok let spustia* (Burdened with Evil, or Forty Years Later), in *Arkadii Strugatskii, Boris Strugatskii. Izbrannoe* (Moscow: Moskovskii rabochii, 1990), 484 639.

16. The capital cyrillic letter "Z" (first letter of the Russian word for "evil") looks much like the Arabic numeral three. A Russian reader might confuse the two.

17. George Anderson, *The Legend of the the Wandering Jew* (Providence: Brown University Press, 1965), 12 14.

18. V. V. Bartol'd, "Museilima," in *Sochineniia. Raboty po istorii islama i arabskogo khalifata,* vol. 6 (Moscow: Akademiia Nauk, 1966): 549 574.

19. Dale Eickelman, "Musaylima: an Approach to the Social Anthropology of Seventh-Century Arabia," *Journal of the Economic and Social History of the Orient* 10 (July 1967): 45.

Chapter Three

Apocalyptic Settings

On the threshold of the 21st century. A communal apartment. Misery. Above it all, written in black marker pen on the white tile walls of the kitchen, a reminder: "Lasciate ogni speranza"
—Strugatsky, *Burdened with Evil*

Dantean Circles of Hell

The Doomed City was completed in 1975, but first published in 1988. It is a novel in six parts. Each part corresponds to a stage in the development of the hero's consciousness. In fact, the hero's spiritual journey begins only after his death, since the city in which the novel's action takes place is located in the afterlife. We learn on the first pages of the novel that all the inhabitants of the city made a choice at the moment of their death to participate in an Experiment, whereupon they were transferred directly into the city. As a result, the city's inhabitants obviously derive from different geographical locations and different moments in history, although they all speak Russian and they all have arrived from relatively recent—post- World War II—history. Most of the city's inhabitants have no recollection of their former lives; the exceptions, who figure in the discussion below, prove the rule; hence their enormous significance as bearers of memory and culture.

The city's social and political culture is clearly modelled on elements of Soviet and Chinese-style totalitarianism mixed with Nazi fascism. Within this culture, there are dissenting groups, as well as possibilities to cooperate and rise to the top. The main protagonist, Andrei, enters life-after-death as a lowly garbage collector, along with an American and a Chinese man. He acquires a mistress who obviously left the "real" world as a spoiled citizen of a decadent Scandinavian society. The American turns out to be a dissenter, and is eventually killed, while Andrei is rotated upwards through the city's hierarchy of jobs, to become the editor of an important newspaper, and later—after a coup during which the fascists come to power—a high-placed government functionary. His rise to the top is chronicled in the first four of the book's six parts. His accumulation of power and status is passive; he neither condones violence and racism, nor does he take an informed stand against it. His former mistress, now his wife, is equally guilty of Andrei's great crime: unthinking conformity. Only the witty and eccentric Jewish intellectual, Andrei's friend Izya Katsman, has managed to survive all the vicissitudes of the city's political climate by adroitly manipulating his image as "court jester." His slovenly dress, over-excitable behavior, and stereotyped mannerisms provide a safe, humorous front for his tremendous erudition and intellectual curiosity.

In part 5 of *The Doomed City*, Andrei leaves his post as a functionary in the fascist regime to embark upon an expedition to the end of the world ("the Anti-city") with Izya. In part 6, he has come full circle, as the plot closes in upon itself in the manner of a Moebius strip: Both Andrei and Izya die in the final leg of their journey, but reappear, in the last scene, in their native city of Leningrad. The enigmatic "Supervisor," who has appeared to Andrei in crucial moments of his journey, is ready to greet him when he arrives back from the underworld:

> "Well, Andrei," said the voice of the Supervisor in a rather ceremonial tone. "You have passed through the first circle. The lamp under a green glass shade was switched on, and its circle of light fell on a fresh copy of "Leningrad Pravda" with the large headline: Leningraders' love for Stalin has no limits." . . .
> Andrei smoothed the paper absent-mindedly and said:
> "The first? Why the first?"
> "Because many still lie ahead," answered the voice of the Supervisor.
> Trying not to look in the direction the voice was coming from, Andrei got up and leaned against the cupboard to look out the window. The black well of the courtyard, weakly lit by the yellow squares of windows, stretched below him and rose above him. Somewhere high above, in the already dark sky, the Vega star shone. It was absolutely impossible to leave all of this again, and absolutely impossible—even more so!—to remain amidst of this. Now. After all that had happened.
> "Izya! Izya!" shouted a woman in the well. "Izya, time for dinner! . . . Children, have you seen Izya?"

Children's voices down below began to shout:

"Izzie! Katsman! Come on, your Mom's calling you...!"

Andrei pressed his face to the window with all his might, trying to peer into the darkness. But all he could see were indistinct shadows, sliding along the wet, black pit of the well between towering piles of timber logs.[1]

In the course of the novel, Andrei has been guided through several circles of hell by his Supervisor, only to return to his earthly existence "after all that had happened." On the other hand, the final scene obviously precedes the action of the novel, since in it Izya is still a child, and Leningraders still harbor a boundless love for Stalin. Andrei dies shortly thereafter,— perhaps in one of Stalin's camps "between towering piles of timber logs"—at which point he arrives at the first page of the novel, as a garbage collector in *The Doomed City*.

The Supervisor's reference to Dante's concentric circles of Hell acquires a new dimension of meaning in the distinct setting of a Leningrad apartment complex in the late 1930s. A comparison of the city's nineteenth-century Russian architecture, with tall, solid buildings surrounding a central courtyard, to the vertical structure of Dante's Hell, suggests a number of parallels. Dante's hell, a funnel-shaped pit, represents the deepening possibilities of evil within the soul. Superimposing Dante's and the Strugatskys' topographies of evil, ordinary street-life in the city ruled by Stalin becomes equivalent to the floor of hell, except for the implication that the depths of the well lie even lower than Andrei's view to the ground. The pit of hell is in the vision of a labor camp: "indistinct shadows sliding between towering piles of timber logs."[2] On the other hand, the Vega star high above the steep sides of the buildings corresponds to the "bright planet" which gives the poet Dante hope, when he first strays from the Right Path into the Dark Forest which leads to Hell. Andrei's detour onto the path to Hell can be compared to the beginning of Dante's journey through the Underworld:

Midway this way of life we're bound upon
I woke to find myself in a dark wood,
Where the right road was wholly lost and gone.
. . .

How I got into it I cannot say,
Because I was so heavy and full of sleep
When first I stumbled from the narrow way.
                    (1.1 3,10 13)[3]

In part 1, chapter 3 of *The Doomed City*, Andrei has just been catapulted out of a fantastic "Red House" onto a square in the city. The "Red House" appears in a different location in the city on different nights; it seems to exist at will in different places at different times. Although the bad injury Andrei has suffered on his forehead is unambiguously painful, the reality, or irreality, of the circumstances in which he incurred the injury is very ambiguous. He would like to believe that he was *not* inside the migratory "Red House":

> He was sitting on a bench in front of that idiotic cement basin of the fountain, and holding a damp rag which had already become warm to an enormous bump above his right eye. It was painful to the touch, and his head hurt so much he was afraid that he had cracked his skull, . . . Although, as a matter of fact, all this was perhaps for the better. All this lent what had happened the definitive outlines of raw reality. There was no House . . . but simply a man was wandering in the dark, he started to get drowsy and went and crashed over a low cement barrier right into this idiotic pit, cracking his stupid head and everything else on the cold cement floor. . . . (268)

Andrei's "realistic" version of his misadventure is partially prefigured by its Dantean source. We know from part 1 of the novel that Andrei arrived in *The Doomed City* "midway through his life." In part 2, he is lost in the dark, and due to extreme fatigue, he stumbles over a cement obstacle—the modern urban equivalent of a tree root in the forest, as well as an inverted reference to the divine fountain of paradise. The physical parallels in the two stories are made significant by parallels on the spiritual plane. Although Dante's Lower Hell is populated by historical or legendary personages who are suffering the consequences of their various willed perversions, they are also *allegorical* figures representing the potential for evil inherent in the poet's own soul, and within any individual soul. It is a gross, but not inaccurate simplification of the allegory to say that until each individual recognizes the hell within, it will be impossible for any community, or country, or humankind as a whole to achieve the harmony of Paradise—in secular terms, social utopia. Virgil is chosen to accompany Dante in his journey through Hell, because he represents the composite cultural and artistic achievements of Western civilization. His art and philosophy and morality cannot in and of themselves open the gates of Heaven, but they can awaken and guide the sinful soul onto the path of righteousness and salvation.

Dante's epic poem is also a political jeremiad, aimed at the critical sociopolitical situation in thirteenth-century Italy. In her introduction to *The Divine Comedy*, Dorothy Sayers formulates the point of the historical Dante's political concerns as "a protest against that drive towards theocracy . . . [which he viewed as] an attempt to establish the Kingdom of God here and now as an ecclesiastical-political structure" (46). The great twofold pattern which unfolds in Dante's epic poem confirms a view of history as a process of redemption within time and salvation as a process of redemption outside of time. Dante rails against the essentially humanistic attempt to locate the Kingdom of God not in eternity, but in time. Thus, as one of the Strugatskys' characters shrewdly comments, "the ideas behind communism have much in common with the ideas of early Christianity." Let us hypothesize, then, that in *The Doomed City*, the Strugatskys have chosen to guide the protagonist through Dante's circles of hell again, in order to arrive at some explanation for humanity's failure, in the twentieth century, to exorcise the roots of fascism, Stalinism, and racism from its soul—and from the reality of its temporal "Kingdoms." Further significant parallels between the two texts highlight the ironic discrepancies between Dante's and the Strugatskys' cosmologies.

As Andrei is regaining consciousness on the edge of the cement fountain, his first "guide" appears in the person of a learned old man, whose speech confirms the intertextual relationship between Dante's *Divine Comedy* and *The Doomed City*.

> "Well now," said the little man in a clear grandfatherly voice. "What will happen next?"
> "I don't know," said Andrei after some thought. "Maybe something else creepy will show up. After all, the Experiment is an Experiment. It will last for a long time."

"It will last forever," said the old man. "All religions agree that it lasts forever."

"Religion has nothing to do with this," Andrei objected.

"You still think that way even now?" the old man was surprised.

"Of course. And I always did."

"Fine, we won't get into that for the time being. The Experiment is an Experiment. . . . But I have something else in mind. Why are we left with free will, even here? You would think that here in the kingdom of absolute evil, where the gates are inscribed *Abandon all hope. . .*"

Andrei waited for a continuation, but none was forthcoming, so he said:

"You have a strange conception of things. This isn't the kingdom of absolute evil. This is more like chaos, which we are called upon to bring to order. How can we establish order unless we are granted free will?"

"An interesting thought," said the old man upon reflection. "You mean, you propose that we have been given one more chance? Something like serving in a punishment battalion to wash away the blood of our sins on this far outpost of the eternal battleground between good and evil. . ."

"What does evil have to do with it"? objected Andrei, who was becoming somewhat annoyed. "Evil is something intentional. . ."

"You are a Manichaean!" the old man exclaimed.

"I am a Komsomol!" objected Andrei, becoming even more annoyed and experiencing an unusual flood of belief and conviction. "Evil is always a class phenomenon. There is no such thing as evil in general. Here everything is mixed up because of the Experiment. We have been given chaos. Either we capitulate, and return to what we had there—class inequities and all that crap,—or we harness the chaos and turn it into a new, beautiful form of human relationships, known as communism. . ."

For a while the old man maintained a stunned silence.

"Well, I'll be. . ." he said at last with enormous surprise. Who would have thought, who would have guessed. . . Communist propaganda—here! (269-70)

The humor of the situation arises out of the discrepancy between Andrei's perception of where he is and who he is, and the perceptions of the old man, who is "in the know." Andrei naively believes himself to be a Soviet komsomol still in the living ("real") world, whereas the old man knows that they are both shadows in the Afterworld. However, the Strugatskys' Afterworld is not entirely imaginary or fantastic. On the contrary, it is contiguous with Andrei's world and has a palpable quality of empirical reality—it is, after all, physically extant in many works of art. For example, the old man has no trouble identifying the location of the phantasmagoric "Red House" in the temporal world, thereby "rationalizing" its existence in the Afterworld:

> "It's not hard to recognize it, said the old man softly.
> "Before, in that life, I often saw it depicted and described. It is described in great detail in the *Revelations of St. Anthony*. Of course, that particular text has not been canonized, . . . For us Catholics . . . Well, anyway, I've read it. 'A house appeared to me, it was alive and in motion, it made indecent gestures, and I could see through the windows that inside there were people who walked through the rooms, slept, and ate. . .' I can't claim that this is an exact quote, but it's very close. Then, of course, there is Hieronymous Bosch. I would call him Saint Hieronymous Bosch, and I'm very much obliged to him for preparing me for this. . ."—he motioned broadly to his surroundings. . . .
> I recognize a great deal of what I see here, and it pains me to even think of those who have arrived here without understanding, and without the capacity to understand, where they are. A tortuous incomprehension of what surrounds them, compounded by tortuous memories of their sins. Perhaps this is also the great wisdom of the Creator: eternal consciousness of one's sins without the realization that one is being punished. . . . Take, for example, you, young man—for what sins were you hurled into this abyss?"
> "I don't understand what you're talking about," grumbled Andrei. 'Religious fanatics are the last thing we need in this place. . .' he thought to himself. (271-272)

Thus, not only the "Red House," but the entire city, and even its geographical location, has a solid precedent in artistic and cultural icons of Western civilization. The pattern of intertextual allusions is already evident: the setting is prefigured by artistic depictions of the Apocalypse and the Underworld. In the interplay between the Strugatskys' "fantastic" setting and its "real" intertextual precedent, the discrepancy between the two planes of reality is, in fact, neutralized. Both Andrei's perceptions and the old man's perceptions are correct simultaneously: they are living in the Soviet Union in the latter half of the twentieth century, *and* they are living in Hell. If one distills and specifies the source of humor in the Strugatskys' text, one finds that the humor of the situation arises as a kind of inevitable byproduct of the "neutralization" process: the realization that the real and the fantastic—the contemporary reader's world and the "infernos" of world literature—are one and the same thing, evokes the ironic laughter of recognition. As the scene above

continues, Andrei and the old man are approached by the witty
and learned Jew, Izya Katsman.

> Trying to sound as nonchalant as possible, Andrei said:
> "This elderly gentleman considers that all of us here are in hell."
> "The elderly gentleman is absolutely correct," Izya promptly replied,
> and started to snicker. At any rate, if this isn't hell, it is something so
> similar that you can't tell them apart." (274)

It is important to realize that the Strugatskys' allegorical representation of the Soviet Union as "something so similar [to
hell] that you can't tell them apart" is not confined to the
period of Stalinism. Izya is a mere child when Andrei experiences his flashback to the Stalinist past—and the lowest level of
Dante's hell. Most of the fictional Afterworld depicted in the
novel is contemporaneous with the novel's composition, i.e., it
coincides with the Soviet Union of the early 1970s. The following interrogation confirms these dates both by the typical form
of its questions, and the content of Izya's answers.

> "Name? Surname? Patronymic?"
> "Katsman, Joseph Mikhailovich"
> "Year of birth?"
> "Thirty-six."
> "Nationality?"[4]
> "Yes," said Katsman with a snicker. . . .
> "Nationality!"
> "Jewish," answered Izya with disgust.
> "Citizen of what country?"
> "U-S-S-R"
> "Religious preference?"
> "None."
> "Party membership?"
> "None." . . .
> "Year of departure from Earth?"
> "Nineteen sixty-eight."
> "Place of departure?"
> "Leningrad."
> "Reason for departure?"
> "Curiosity."
> (287)

The interrogation is conducted by Andrei, who, as a recently
promoted young prosecutor in part 2, is willing to indict his
best friend in the name of arbitrary laws which he neither

understands nor questions. Despite the interrogation's humorous overtones, within the Dantean context, it locates Andrei—and a whole society—in the lowest circle of hell, reserved for those who commit the sin of treachery. In the course of parts 3, 4, and 5 of the novel, Andrei advances upwards as far as the first circle (part 6).

Whereas Dante's Hell is a vertical structure, the Strugatskys' Hell has horizontal dimensions. Andrei's spiritual journey corresponds roughly with his movement away from the bowels of the city (as a garbage collector), to the suburbs, and, finally, to the uncharted stretch of territory which leads from the city to the Anti-city. Andrei is put in charge of an exploratory expedition destined for the Anti-city. He is provided with civilian troops, and he takes Izya along in the capacity of historian. As Andrei moves further away (laterally) from the city, his capacity to acknowledge and find meaning in the sights of Hell increases. One of the most striking moments in the growth of his awareness occurs when his troops are about to mutiny. The setting is imbued with Boschian motifs, which warrant a separate digression.

Hieronymous Bosch

Whether one interprets Bosch's bizarre images as inspired by medieval heresies, esoteric sects, and alchemy, or, on the contrary, as illustrations of contemporary, i.e., fifteenth century, religious sermons and didactic literature (Bosch scholars stand in opposing camps), there is no question that the central panel of the *Temptation of St. Anthony* triptych is apocalyptic. Since the old man confides to Andrei that the art of Hieronymus Bosch "helped prepare him for life in this city," we can assume that the authors intended the spiritual and physical landscape of the *The Doomed City* to resonate—five centuries later—with the vision of the world described by the medieval Dutch painter. This vision is a quintessentially pessimistic world view, in which man struggles weakly against his evil inclinations, more likely to sink to the level of beasts than to rise with the angels. It is a world of stark dualism between temptations of the Flesh and the Devil and the chaste suffering of a few saints. It is the epitome of what philosophical humanism arose out of, and in con-

tradiction to. Scenes of Boschian evil in *The Doomed City* are
not hard to find: there is debauchery, drunkenness, sexual
promiscuity (Bosch: *The Seven Deadly Sins*) as well as chaotic
rioting and burning villages (Bosch: *The Last Judgment*). Of
course, these are nearly universal images of sin and immanent
apocalypse. Nevertheless, the old man's explicit reference to
Bosch allows one to make more than broadly thematic compar-
isons between the medieval artist's world and the Strugatskys'
modern hell. There are passages in the Strugatskys' prose
which warrant a stylistic comparison with Bosch's half-human,
half-beast, half-mythical monsters, which have been likened to
those of Salvador Dali. In one scene in part 5 of *The Doomed
City*, several soldiers led by a particularly brutish soldier named
"Khnoipek" gang-rape a young retarded girl appropriately
nicknamed "Mymr," since she never articulates anything more
than that syllable. In Andrei's formulation of the meaning of
the incident, the characters' strange names combine to form an
abstract noun—an effective neologism which represents the
"half-human, half-beast" hordes. Another neologism derives
from the word for belly-button ("pupok"), and would seem to be
peculiarly appropriate also to Bosch's frequent motif of bloated
bellies—gluttonous bellies, pregnant (sinfully) bellies, and cock-
roach-like bellies.

> Here we come straight to the question of the role of God and the Devil
> in history. . . . that God took chaos into His hands and organized it,
> while the Devil, on the contrary, always tries to destroy his order. . . .
> On the other hand, what, I ask you, have the most vicious tyrants occu-
> pied themselves with throughout history? They have tried to take pre-
> cisely that chaotic nature in human beings, that self-same amorphous
> knoipekomymriness *[khnoipekomymrost']*, and in all possible ways orga-
> nize it, straighten it out, give it form, line it up—preferably in a single
> column—aim it in a single direction and, in general, counter-abort it,
> or, to put it simply, abort it. *[ukontrapupit', upupit'*: "counter-bud, de-
> belly-button"] (451)

The Strugatskys' grotesque neologisms, like Bosch's visual
images, seem to function here as part of a philosophical ques-
tioning of the meaning of chaos, and the devil's role in history.

The Apocalyptic Horseman

As far as I know, this is the only monument to a man on an armored car that exists in the world. In this respect alone, it is a symbol of a new society. The old society used to be represented by men on horseback.

—Joseph Brodsky, "A Guide to a Renamed City"

The presence of the Avenging Horseman in Russian apocalyptic literature has been enormous, ever since Pushkin's poem *The Bronze Horseman* imbued the founding of Petersburg by Peter the Great with mythic significance. David Bethea's study of *The Shape of the Apocalypse in Modern Russian Literature* gives much consideration to the persistent, but changing image of the Apocalyptic Horse(man). As might be expected, the Apocalyptic Horseman also makes his appearance in *The Doomed City*.

> Boom, boom, boom—he could hear it very close by, and the earth shook beneath his feet. Suddenly there was silence. Andrei immediately looked out [from around the corner] again. He saw: at the nearest intersection, its head reaching up to the third floor, looms a dark figure. A statue. An old-fashioned metal statue. That same old character with the frog face—only now he stood tensely thrust forward, jutting out his ample chin. One arm rested behind his back, and the other—either admonishing, or pointing to the skies—was raised up with the index finger extended. (442)

In this striking image, the most ominous features of the equestrian statue of Peter the Great are conflated with the statue of Lenin standing on top of an armored car in his iconographic "Finland Station" pose. Like Pushkin's Bronze Horseman, the statue Andrei sees has assumed enormous proportions and terrifies the little man with his thundering steps. Like the statue of Lenin at Finland Station, "he is depicted in the usual quasi-romantic fashion, with his hand poking into the air, supposedly addressing the masses. . . ." [5] Moreover, the statue Andrei sees is standing at an intersection: symbolically, at the crossroads of history. Unlike his predecessors, though, the Strugatskys' statue no longer presides over the spirit of St. Petersburg or Leningrad; he presides in one of the circles of Hell. The bronze image of Peter I *cum* Lenin is simply pointing; a bankrupt gesture in Hell.

The circle of Hell in which the Strugatskys have situated Russia's great reformers (Peter the Great, Lenin) is the seventh circle—the City of Dis. In Dante's poem, when the poets enter the City of Dis, they find themselves on a great plain covered with the burning tombs of the Heretics:

> For strewn among the tombs tall flames flared fierce,
>   Heating them so white-hot as never burned
>   Iron in the forge of any artificers.
>
> The grave-slabs all were thrown back and upturned,
>   And from within came forth such fearful crying,
> 'Twas plain that here sad tortured spirits mourned.
>   (9.118-123)

When Andrei and Izya walk into the city inhabited by the metal statue, they come upon a great square strewn with the pedestals of departed statues. The souls who have wandered out of their flaming tombs in Dante's Dis have likewise wandered off their monuments (gravestones) into the scorching city visited by Andrei and Izya:

> They [Andrei and Izya] walked on and on, growing delirious from the heat. . . .
>   Then they came out onto a square. They had never come across a square like this before. It looked as if a remarkable forest had been razed. Pedestals stuck out like stumps. . . . pedestals of stone, iron, sandstone, marble. . . . But all of the pedestals were empty. (445)

Andrei eventually encounters all the statues—presumably, the souls of Heretics—who are aware of their rejection of God, but deliberately commit the sins represented in the lower circles of Hell: Violence (or Bestiality) and Fraud (or Malice). In their company, he attempts to make a speech in which he defines the spiritual boundary between deliberately willed evil, and the lesser sins of Incontinence (circles three, four, five, and six) and passive (unwitting) Unbelief (circle two). In other words, the Strugatskys' imagery—incomplete gravestones on a scorching plain—and the subject of Andrei's speech to the statues correspond to both the physical and spiritual setting of Dante's City of Dis on the boundary between the Upper and Lower circles of Hell. Andrei's pseudo-scientific vocabulary, super-imposed upon the colloquial speech and world view of his former Soviet incarnation, is woefully inadequate to the task:

> "... it's not important whether [we have in mind] a military court in the field or a jury court, the secret court of the Inquisition, or a lynch law, or the so-called court of honor. Not to mention the comrades' courts, and other such things. It was necessary to find a form for the organization of chaos, consisting of such sexual and digestive organs as Khnoipek as well as Mymr—a form for this tavern of a universe, in which at least some part of the functions invested in the above-mentioned external courts would be transferred to the court within each individual. That is when the category of greatness became apt and appropriate!" (449)

Once Andrei has made the realization that the "category of greatness" applies to individual morality, rather than to those who seek to conquer or legislate in the name of some abstract morality, he is ready to leave the Heretics' city and proceed, in the company of his enlightened guide Izya, toward the first circle. By the end of the novel, both Andrei and Izya have earned their place among the Unbaptized and the Virtuous Pagans in the first circle, or Limbo: Izya the Jew because his only "sin" is not having been baptized, and Andrei because his only remaining "sin" is his upbringing outside of the Church (in the atheist Soviet State). By the end of the novel, Andrei has acquired an understanding of the importance of memory and culture. He has joined the ranks of Dante's Virtuous Pagans as an active, conscious participant in the building, preservation, and appreciation of the "Temple of Culture,"—as Izya calls the edifice constructed out of the best of human philosophy, morality, poetry, science, art, and imagination. Without the Temple of Culture, there is no hope for individual or collective salvation.

The Metaphysical Landscape

The Strugatskys' novel *A Lame Fate* can be read as a continuing dialog with the visionary, apocalyptic literature of Russia's Silver Age, and with Bulgakov's *The Master and Margarita* in particular. The writers who formulated their apocalyptic foreboding in response to the 1917 Revolution did not live to see most of them realized during the Stalinist Terror and the Holocaust.

The Strugatskys' generation is, in this sense, a post-apocalypse generation, born after the Revolution which promised the millennium (in the form of a "radiant communist future") had set the course of history backwards in the opposite direction. Thus, while making reference to the literary forms and eschatological views of their literary predecessors, the Strugatskys go beyond them to create a form and an "eschatology" unique to the experience of Soviet intellectuals who came of age during and after Stalin's reign. In order to understand how myths about the end of History have changed in the Russian imagination during the Soviet period, it is necessary to look at how the image of the apocalyptic city has been modified and changed.

During roughly the same period in the early seventies that the Strugatskys were working on *The Doomed City*, they were also drafting another novel called *A Lame Fate*. The narrator-protagonist of this novel was cast as a Soviet writer whose apocalyptic masterpiece, *The Ugly Swans* (sometimes under the title *A Time of Rain*) was originally interpolated into the frame chapters as a novel-within-a novel. For the sake of clarity, I will continue to refer to the frame story only as *A Lame Fate,* and to the novel-within-the novel as *The Ugly Swans.*

Felix Alexandrovich Sorokin, the narrator and main protagonist of *A Lame Fate,* is an outwardly successful Moscow writer, whose formerly robust constitution is starting to show signs of an ailing old age. The writer's physical premonitions of the end—however hypochondriac they may be—are reflected in the setting of the city in which he lives, and in the setting of the city which he writes about. In this sense, the Strugatskys add to the repertoire of depictions in Russian literature of the "threshold city": the geographical focal point on Earth of the final battle between the Savior and the antichrist.[6] For Pushkin, Dostoevsky, Bely, Blok, and Brodsky, the imperial capital of Petersburg embodies the dualities whose ultimate confrontation signals the Apocalypse. For Bulgakov and Pasternak, the apocalyptic city is the "fallen" Third Rome of Moscow. In *The Shape of the Apocalypse in Modern Russian Literature,* David Bethea notes that the "threshold city" is the place "where the modern seer, straddling two different temporalities, catches a glimpse of an otherworldly order in the midst of worldly chaos and revolution" (Bethea, 45). The "modern seer" is, in effect, a "threshold protagonist,"—one whose idiocy (Dostoevsky's *Idiot*), androgyny (Bely's Nikolai), lunacy (Bulgakov's Master), inspiration (Blok's lyrical narrator; Pasternak's Zhivago), or internal exile (Brodsky) afford him a vision of the "no-man's-land" between the profane and the sacred essence of the city. Both inspiration and, ironically, censorship, allow the hero of the Strugatskys' *A Lame Fate* to straddle several temporalities at once. The concept of temporality must be broadened here to mean something akin to Bakhtin's "chronotope," i.e., a time-space zone characterized by an inherent set of ethical assumptions. In short, Sorokin is a threshold protagonist—a writer who functions both within the mainstream literary establishment *and* in opposition to it. The city he lives in is an apocalyptic, fallen city, and the cities he writes about are threshold cities, where an age-old struggle between opposite poles is still being played out. Both the realistic and the fantastic planes in the novel belong to the genre of Apocalypse, so that the boundary between the two is completely permeable. Sorokin's mimetic description of contemporary Moscow *byt* is freely invaded by fantastic characters and events from another, symbolic reality. Likewise, the fictional landscape Sorokin envisions in the novel he is writing is also the symbolic geographical embodiment of a metaphysical problem.

The fifty-six year old Moscow writer (Sorokin) who is the main protagonist of *A Lame Fate* tells us that at one time he served as a interpreter and translator of Japanese. Thus, the approximate age and vocation of the narrator are those of one of the authors, Arkady Strugatsky. Both the narrator's matter-of-fact, colloquial style and the autobiographical facts attributed to him belie the reader's expectations of a fantastic plot. Sorokin mentions that he is a member of the Writer's Union, and that he frequents the exclusive Club where members of that Union are privileged to eat and drink (usually to an excess). He candidly confesses that he pays for this and other privileges by writing literature acceptable to the prevailing interpretation of what comprises the official genre of Socialist Realism. In his private, unofficial life he is working on another novel which includes elements of the fantastic, science fiction, and apocalyptic motifs. He keeps this manuscript in a blue folder in his desk drawer, as he has no hope of publishing it in the Soviet Union. In a continuing dialog with Bulgakov, the Strugatskys cast Sorokin as a contemporary Master, struggling to finish his literary and philosophical masterpiece fully aware that "during my lifetime it will never be published, because I don't see a single publisher on the horizon whom it would be possible to convince that my visions are important for at least a dozen other people in the world besides myself."[7]

Thus, semi-autobiographical reminiscences, excerpts from drafts of actual Strugatsky novels, and detailed naturalistic descriptions of Writer's Club meals and conversation form the realistic backdrop in *A Lame Fate* for a zany and incomplete science fiction plot. The narrator becomes implicated against his will in a conspiracy of five immortals who jealously guard their limited source of the elixir of life. As an unwitting sixth person to have found out about the elixir, the narrator's life may be in danger. He is followed about the city by a ominous character in a checkered jacket, all the more threatening in light of his intertextual relationship to Koroviev-Fagot in *The Master and Margarita*. (In that novel, when the "checkered citizen" materializes before Berlioz's eyes, it is the first signal of the editor's impending doom, to which the "checkered citizen" is, indeed, the only witness.) Furthermore, Sorokin is baited in a cafe by a fallen angel who offers him the musical score for the trumpet call at the Last Judgment; and finally, he receives a threat note from extraterrestrial aliens. None of these science fiction motifs is developed any further. The gang of immortals and their elixir disappear, and the aliens never materialize to force the demands made in their note.[8] Meanwhile, a second science fiction subplot motivates the protagonist's actions and spiritual development in a more indirect, but significant way. In this subplot, the Writer's Union has requested that all members bring a sample of their writing to the Linguistics Institute on Bannaya street. The linguists have at their disposal a new super-computer capable of providing an objective evaluation of any work of literature. The machine is programmed to determine in quantitative terms the artistic value of a given work.

Distracted by his run-ins with the immortal mafia, and sub-liminally anxious about submitting his art to scientific analysis, the narrator consistently "forgets" to bring in a sample of his work to the Institute. As this subplot is being formulated at the beginning of the novel, it is presented as science fiction in a lightly satirical vein:

> Of course, there is nothing so great about lying like a log in the path of scientific-technological progress; on the other hand—well, we're only human: either I happen to be on Bannaya street and remember that I should stop in at the Linguistics Institute, but my manuscripts are not with me; or I am carrying my manuscripts under my arm, headed for the Institute, and for some strange reason I end up not on Bannaya street, but, on the contrary, at the Club. My explanation for these enigmatic deviations is that it is impossible to consider this scheme—as most schemes devised by our administrative department—with the nec-essary seriousness. Really now, what kind of linguistic entropy can pos-sibly exist in our Moscow? And what does it have to do with me? (9)

The serious answer to the narrator's half-facetious question lies encoded in the various settings depicted in different layers of the novel. The analyses below show how the urban setting becomes one of the main protagonists of the novel, mediating between the fantastic and the realistic layers of the plot. In its capacity as mediator between contemporary *byt* and the apoca-lyptic motif, the setting is endowed with great thematic impor-tance.

The physical setting of the Strugatskys' fictional world is at once both nauseatingly familiar,—and strangely apocalyptic:

> I was sitting by the window. . . sipping warm "bzhni" mineral water with disgust. . . . Outside it was snowing heavily, cars were creeping anx-iously along the highway, huge snow drifts were building up on the shoulders; beyond, through the curtain of blowing snow, one could make out the mournfully black clumps of bare trees and bristling spots and lines of bushes on the vacant lot.
>
> Moscow was snowed in.
>
> Moscow was snowed in like some god-forsaken railway stop out beyond Aktyubinsk. (3)

In these opening paragraphs of *A Lame Fate*, realistic details are provided literally *ad nauseam*, as the protagonist—who suf-fers from pre-ulcer symptoms, as we find out later—sips a salu-brious mineral water with disgust, and watches Moscow traffic coming to a confused halt in the midst of a heavy winter storm.[9] To the average Russian reader, everything from the taste of "bzhni" mineral water to the haphazard flora of Moscow's un-landscaped, vacant urban lots is so familiar that the scene could pass as a photographic likeness of everyday, common experience. However, with equal facility one could imagine that this frame was taken from a post-holocaust film. The landscape is real and specific, but it is also imbued with the presence of another symbolic and timeless reality that lurks behind it. The trees are naked and black. There are no people visible, and even their cars crawl anxiously through the elemental rage of nature. The first chapter is subtitled *"purga,"* which is a strong storm or blizzard, and it is structurally and semantically opposed to the last chapter, which is subtitled *Exodus.* The eschatological overtones of the latter term strengthen the apocalyptic mood of the former. The view from the window is onto a vacant lot. The selection of images and "verbal lighting" creates an impression of darkness and abandonment. The figure of speech in the last line strikes home as a literal designation: *a god-forsaken place.*

The apocalyptic mood hinted at in the imagery used to describe the narrator's urban neighborhood is intensified when the narrator goes to a local cafe to breakfast. The appearance of the cafe in which the narrator breakfasts is irrelevant to the formation of the plot, which only requires that he be eating at a table where one seat is empty, allowing a new protagonist to approach and strike up a conversation. Nevertheless, the cafe is described in striking detail. The name of the cafe, "The Pearl Oyster," conjures up associations with the seaside, romantic exoticism, or, at the very least, something bright and delicate hidden in its shell. Instead, the cafe's exterior most resembles a low-slung artillery bunk:

> it reminds me of the artillery bunk "Million" near the Finnish border, crushed by a direct hit of a thousand-kilogram bomb: slabs of tedious gray cement stick out in all directions, connected by knots of rusty iron siding, which in the architect's conception are supposed to represent seaweed. The windows are imbedded in ferro-concrete reinforcements running along [the facade] at the level of the sidewalk. (188)

Here the architecture of the narrator's world becomes in and of itself an incarnation of that world's epistemological presuppositions. For if architecture, like language, is the "being" which determines consciousness, then the authors mean to show us that we live in a world of apocalyptic ugliness, a rusty imitation of nature, unredeemed, for the time being, by any evidence of humanity's pretensions to a spiritual dimension. The behavior of the waiter inside of the cafe is entirely appropriate: "he managed a strange combination of nonchalance and sleepy moroseness" (188). Thus, the cafe "The Pearl Oyster," at once humorous and endearing by its very familiarity—for most cafes in Moscow are staffed by surly waiters and have the same two things on the menu ("beef stroganoff and meat baked in a crock")—also provides the symbolic context for the events which befall the narrator within.

While Sorokin is breakfasting in "The Pearl Oyster," a disheveled hunchback with golden wavy hair joins him at his table and introduces himself as a fallen angel who has in his possession the musical score for the trumpet call at the Last Judgment. At this point, there is tension between two possible ways of interpreting the "angel's" presence. The hunchback might be a mentally imbalanced young man impressing his delusions upon reluctant diners in a Moscow cafe. On the other hand, in a city imbued with apocalyptic imagery, it seems more likely that the hunchback with golden curls really *is* a fallen angel.

The fallen angel is no more and no less a part of empirical reality than any other character in the story, almost all of whom freely cross the boundary from one literary existence to another. Sorokin is the narrator of a fictional novel, in which he reads and writes fiction which exists in the empirical world. His notebooks contain the text for *The Ugly Swans* and drafts for *The Doomed City,* and his own reading material includes, for example, a short story by the Japanese author Akutagawa. Akutagawa's fantastic tale describes a machine which measures a writer's talent. In *A Lame Fate,* Akutagawa's literary invention becomes as much a part of Sorokin's "real" world as the hard-boiled eggs and fruit kefir he usually has for breakfast:

Menzura Zoila, by Akutagawa, written back in 1916, and translated into Russian already in the mid-thirties! It is impossible to invent anything new. Anything new you think up has either been thought of before, or it actually exists in real life (73).[10]

The disheveled young hunchback who sells Sorokin the score for the Last Judgement trumpet call also derives from another story, one which is relatively hard to translate, as he himself is disarmingly aware:

> The deal he was going to make with me was this: for only five rubles he was offering the full, unabridged version of the score for the Trumpet Call at the Last Judgment. He had personally translated the original into modern musical notation. Where did he get the original? That was a long story; furthermore, it was difficult to relate in commonly understood terms. (191)

Despite his biblical origins, the fallen angel is subject to the same laws of reality—and banality—as the narrator, the other diners in the cafe, and the other citizens of Moscow:

> He ended up here, down below, without means for a living, literally with just what he had in his pockets. It was almost impossible to find work, since naturally he had no identification documents. (191)

Subjecting an otherworldly being to petty discomforts and inconveniences which all mere mortals must endure is a device of carnivalesque humor. This particular "angel," moreover, smells as if he had spent the night in a chicken coop, "enveloping [Sorokin] with a medley of smells from the chicken coop and beer barrel. . ." (191). The humor cuts two ways, though. On the one hand, the travesty elicits the comic incongruity of a deity—even a fallen one—having to "rough it" as a mortal; on the other hand, there is the frightening implication that even the gods are not a match for ordinary twentieth-century bureaucracy. The travesty continues later on, when Sorokin's neighbor, a professional musician, returns the Last Judgment score to Sorokin with a look of tragic hopelessness on his countenance, as if he had just heard the sound of imminent apocalypse:

> [I saw in the doorway] an enormous, veined, light-blue nose over thick mustaches parted in the middle, [I saw] pale trembling lips and dark,

melancholy eyes, filled with tears and despair. The fatal notes were rolled up in a tube and he clutched them convulsively to his breast. He was silent, and I was ceased with such terrible premonitions, that it took my breath away. . . .

"Listen," he croaked, tearing his hands from his face and burying them in the thick wooly hair behind his ears, "Spartak" [Moscow soccer team] bit the dust again! Now what are we going to do, uh?" (219)

On the level of contemporary *byt*, the Strugatskys consistently devalorize the apocalyptic motif. As in *The Master and Margarita*, however, the device of familiarizing the presence of evil does not necessarily provide "comic relief." On the contrary, players in the apocalyptic scenario have lost their grand and cosmic significance and become frighteningly banal and . . . neighborly.

For the narrator of *A Lame Fate*, the consequences of Nietzsche's pronouncement at the end of the nineteenth century that "God is dead" have been compounded by almost a century of repression under an ideological system which moved in to fill the void left in God's absence. The Strugatskys' modern Master grew up as part of that generation in which the potential for evil still depicted by Bulgakov as a vaudeville romp by Woland and his cohorts through Moscow of the 1930s—was realized in the forms Bulgakov satirically envisioned: censorship, the political use of psychiatry, mass indoctrination, and the triumph of scientific atheism are things which Sorokin accepts as mundane reality. Hence, his matter-of-fact brooding on the degradation of art in the centrally planned official culture of the Soviet Union—

Even if I write that [film] script, so what? So it will be accepted, and a young, energetic, and inevitably stupid film director will barge into my life. He will begin to edify me with respectful, but impudent insistence that film is his language, that in film the most important thing is the image, and not the word; he will inevitably begin to throw around homegrown aphorisms such as "not a shot on native soil" and other faddish phrases. What do I care about his petty career maneuvers, when I know beforehand that the film will be shitty and that during the studio previews I will struggle with the impulse to jump up and demand that they remove my name from the credits. (122)

On the nature of censorship and the reading public he is even more pessimistic:

Of course, after the death of an author we sometimes publish some rather curious pieces of his work, as if death had cleansed them of their limber ambiguity, unnecessary allusions, and pernicious subtexts. As if uncontrollable associations die together with their author. Perhaps, perhaps. . . .

Who cares about Sorokin, F. A.? For instance, right now it's morning. Who, among the ten million inhabitants of Moscow, woke up this morning and thought of Tolstoy, L. N.? Other than school children cramming for a lesson on *War and Peace*. A mover of souls. A commander of minds. The mirror of the Russian Revolution. Maybe he ran away from Yasnaya Polyana precisely because in the end this simple and deadening thought occurred to him.

But he was a believer, I [Sorokin] suddenly realized. For him it was much, much easier. Whereas, we know for certain: there is nothing BEFORE and nothing AFTER. A familiar despair swept over me. Between two NOTHINGS there is a weak little spark, and that's our whole existence for you. . . . In fact, whether you built a unique theorem of mathematical infinity or whether you built a dacha from stolen materials is irrelevant, because there is only NOTHINGNESS BEFORE and NOTHINGNESS AFTER, and your life seems full of meaning only up until the moment that you recognize this. (124)

Sorokin's self-indulgent whining is gradually transformed into a new artistic sensibility. He gropes at the boundary between two eras—the religious and the secular—when he speculates that, although Lev Tolstoy had already sensed the meaningless of all life, he was still part of a religious society; the fabric of belief still enveloped more and was less torn. When Sorokin translates his philosophical nihilism into an artistic image, though, he produces a sketch for the landscape of *The Doomed City:*

I watched how in the usual place—always in the same place, a raspberry disk slowly begins to glow. At first the disk shimmers, [...] it is infused with orange, then yellow, than a white light [which is] impossible to look into. A new day begins, . . . and the City arises as if out of nowhere—bright and colorful, stripped with bluish shadows, huge, spread out—multi-storied buildings stacked up, building upon building, and not a single building looks like the others. . . A scorching Yellow Wall becomes visible in the East. It reaches up to the very sky, to unbelievable heights, and it is fraught with crevices and cracks and covered with reddish clumps of lichen. . . . To the left, beyond the roofs of houses, looms a blue-green nothingness, as if there were a sea, but there is no sea. It is a ravine, an unfathomable blue-green void, a blue-green nothingness, an abyss going down to unfathomable depths.

Eternal nothingness to the left and eternal matter to the right, and it is impossible to understand these two eternities. One can only get used to them. And they do—the people whom I place inside this city on a narrow shelf—only five versts in width—between two eternities.[11]

From this description of the landscape, it is immediately evident that the *The Doomed City* is yet another incarnation of Russia's threshold city—St. Petersburg (Leningrad). St. Petersburg is located geographically on the threshold between the vast expanse of the Russian continent stretching to the East, and the foggy blue-green waters of the Finnish Gulf visible to the West. The city's symbolic location in the tradition of Russian literature may be briefly summed up by the following excerpt from Malmstad and Maguire's introduction to Bely's *Petersburg*:

> Writers of the eighteenth century tended to see Petersburg as a magnificent monument to the power of human reason and will: it was a planned city, founded in 1703 and built on a trackless bog. Part 1 of Pushkin's *The Bronze Horseman* (1833) honors this point of view; but part 2 strikes a new note that came to predominate in virtually all literary treatments of Petersburg well into the twentieth century: beneath the "western" facade lay a shadowy world of intangibilities and unrealities, alien to man's reason and apprehensible only to his unconscious being—an "eastern" world, in Russian terminology. It was Petersburg, with its uneasy coexistence of "west" and "east," that appealed to the Russian mind as being emblematic of the larger problem of national identity.[12]

We have previously noted the appearance of the Bronze Horseman in *The Doomed City*. In Sorokin's draft version of the city's setting, the formal reference to Bely's *Petersburg* is made explicit in the images of a) the sun rising over the city (and striking the needle of the Admiralty at the beginning of Nevsky Prospect), and b) the proximity of an unfathomable blue-green presence just beyond the city's multi-storied and rectilinear architecture. The description of Apollon Apollonovich's early morning ride to work through the city in the first chapter of Bely's novel should be used as a basis for a thematic comparison to the Strugatskys version as well; therefore, it is reproduced here at some length:

> Apollon Apollonovich Ableukhov was gently rocking on the satin seat cushions. He was cut off from the scum of the streets by four perpendicular walls. Thus he was isolated from people and from the red covers of the damp trashy rags on sale right there at this intersection.

Proportionality and symmetry soothed the senator's nerves, which had been irritated both by the irregularity of his domestic life and by the futile rotation of our wheel of state.

His tastes were distinguished by their harmonious simplicity.

Most of all he loved the rectilineal prospect; this prospect reminded him of the flow of time between the two points of life. [sic]

There the houses merged cubelike into a regular, five-story row. This row differed from the line of life: for many a wearer of diamond-studded decorations, as for so many other dignitaries, the middle of life's road had proven to be the termination of life's journey.

Inspiration took possession of the senator's soul whenever the lac-quered cube cut along the line of the Nevsky: there the numeration of the houses was visible. And the circulation went on. There, from there, on clear days, from far, far away, came the blinding blaze of the golden needle, the clouds, the crimson ray of the sunset. There, from there, on foggy days—nothing, no one.

And what was there were lines: the Neva and the islands. Probably in those distant days, when out of the mossy marshes rose high roofs and masts and spires, piercing the dank greenish fog in jags—

—on his shadowy sails the Flying Dutchman winged his way toward Petersburg from there, from the leaden expanses of the Baltic and German Seas, in order here to erect, by delusion, his misty lands and to give the name of islands to the wave of onrushing clouds.

Apollon Apollonovich did not like the islands: the population there was industrial and coarse. There the many-thousand human swarm shuffled in the morning to the many-chimneyed factories. The inhabitants of the islands are reckoned among the population of the Empire; the general census has been introduced among them as well.

Apollon Apollonovich did not wish to think further. The islands must be crushed! Riveted with the iron of the enormous bridge, skewered by the arrows of the prospects...

While gazing dreamily into that illimitability of mists, the states-man suddenly expanded out of the black cube of the carriage in all directions and soared above it. He wanted the carriage to fly for-ward, the prospects to fly to meet him—prospect after prospect, so that the entire spherical surface of the planet should be embraced, as in serpent coils, by blackish gray cubes of houses; so that all the earth, crushed by prospects, in its lineal cosmic flight should inter-sect, with its rectilineal principle, unembraceable infinity. . . .
(*Petersburg,* 10 11)

Bely's *Petersburg* describes the capital of the Russian Empire in 1905, just after the country's humiliating defeat in the Russo-Japanese War, and already on its way to cataclysmic social and political changes, which culminate in the 1917 Revolution. All

the literary myths associated with Peter's city are permeated
with an urgent, apocalyptic significance in Bely's novel. The
Russian intelligentsia's conflicting allegiance to both "western"
rationality and "eastern" Orthodoxy and mysticism leads to a
direct and violent confrontation between those who would
favor "western" democratic principles of government   and
those who would insist on "eastern" principles of autocracy in
order to contain the dreaded upwelling of popular anarchy.
Moreover, the conflict between East and West, spontaneity and
order, religion and rationality, and so forth, is divisive on all
levels: it runs between socio-economic classes, between generations, and between the individual's conscious and subconscious
life. Apollon Apollonovich would seek to transfer the "western"
principle of rationality onto the "eastern" spontaneity of the
masses in order to crush them. Vice versa, his son, a follower
of Cohen and Kant, indulges the "eastern" side of his Russian-
Tartar heritage by dressing in an affectedly oriental fashion
and, in a binge of mystical preoccupation with the nihilistic
premises of gnosticism, he agrees to take part in a
revolutionary terrorist plot. In Bely's *Petersburg*, on the eve of
the Revolution, a bomb must explode and bring an end to the
old order. For, as Berdyaev has pointed out,

> Bely is certainly no enemy of the revolutionary idea. . . . The evil of
> revolution for Bely is generated by the evil of old Russia. Essentially he
> wants to expose artistically the illusory character of the Petersburg
> period of Russian history, of our bureaucratic and intellectual Western-
> ism, just as in *The Silver Dove* he unmasked the darkness and ignorance
> resulting from the Eastern element in our popular life.[13]

Although the turn-of-the-century writers' perception of Russia
poised on the brink between apocalypse and millennium has
gained fresh relevance toward the end of the twentieth century,
the imagery and the terms of the End have changed. First of all,
the decisive, revelatory status of the apocalypse itself has worn
off in the seventy-odd years since the Revolution. Apocalyptic
motifs in the Strugatskys' prose are absorbed into the realistic
description of contemporary *byt;* they are domesticized and triv-
ialized. Mystical and gnostic motifs are also given different

expression in Bely's and the Strugatskys' respective "threshold cities."

In Bely's *Petersburg*, Apollon Apollonovich has a vision of the mystical symbol of the Ouroboros, the serpent who encircles the world, swallowing his own tail. Old Ableukhov's consciousness has temporarily exited his body and merged with the "astral" plane of reality, where the apocalyptic (for Bely) image of "the entire spherical surface of the planet. . . embraced, as in serpent coils, by blackish gray cubes of houses" is realized. Bely's style, which Berdyaev likens to "literary cubism," is organically tied to his own mystical presuppositions, beyond the scope of the present discussion. However, the same gnostic image is projected onto the fantastic landscape of the Strugatskys' *The Doomed City*. Sorokin introduces the gnostic motif by revealing the source of his inspiration:

> I had pasted onto the title page a frayed photo-reproduction: a city on a hill, frozen with fear under heavy night clouds and encircled by a gigantic sleeping serpent with wetly gleaming, smooth skin. (22)

The photo is of a painting by Rerikh depicting the Ouroboros entwined around the threshold city, the microcosm of the world. In the Strugatskys' completed version of *The Doomed City*, Sorokin's picture has been transformed into a dramatic landscape of the edge (end) of the world. The two travellers (Andrei and Izya) from the City are approaching the Anti-city,—and the end of a stage in their spiritual journey:

> They stood on top of an enormous rise. To the left, nothing was visible behind the curtain of swirling dust, and to the right. . . one could see the Yellow Wall—not even and smooth, as it appeared from within the City, but all folded and wrinkled, like the bark of a monstrous tree. Below, in front of them, was the beginning of a white stone field, which stretched out flat as a table. It was not a field of gravel, but a single stone, one vast monolith which stretch out for as far as the eye could see. (479)

According to the novel's Dantean subtext, Andrei and Izya have passed through the first circle, and their ascent through the circles of Hell is over. Thus, they are standing on the edge of the Upper world, which is encircled by the smooth, flat sur face of the primordial serpent. The rugged landscape to the right, "like the bark of a monstrous tree," is reminiscent of the Tree of Life, which is often entwined by the serpent symbolizing eternity. The Ouroboros also symbolizes knowledge, however. Andrei's journey ends here, but he has made it to a new stage of knowledge. Sorokin's own journey toward higher knowledge takes him both through the tradition of Russian literature—as he grapples with the heritage of Bely and Bulgakov in particular—and through the daily grind of Moscow life. The latter, like the former, is imbued with gnostic motifs and a sense of apocalypse.

The hegemony of Socialist Realism in Soviet literature stretched from the early thirties into the first "thaw" in the early sixties. The ideological and aesthetic tenets of Socialist Realism precluded treatment of the apocalyptic theme—if anything, contemporary reality was supposed to resemble the millennium. Therefore, between Bely's masterpiece of apocalyptic foreboding, in which the Russian Revolution is equated with the End of History, and the Strugatskys' contemporary reformulations of that theme, there lie only a few suppressed works which might serve as literary links. One of these—*The Master and Margarita*—will be discussed as an obvious influence on the Strugatskys. The other link between in the tradition of Russian apocalyptic literature is the work of Andrei Platonov.

Platonov's Pit

Direct references to Platonov's work are few and far between in the Strugatskys' novels; although the authors were familiar with Platonov's banned works as early as the 1970s.[14] However, an implicit acknowledgment of Platonov's apocalyptic imagery and language provides a crucial missing link between the grandiose visions of the Symbolists and the ironic vision of the Strugatskys.

The most direct allusion to Platonov in the Strugatskys' works pertains, tellingly, to *The Foundation Pit (Kotlovan)*, the gloomiest of Platonov's novels. Book 2, part 4 of *The Doomed City* opens with a scene of workers digging a foundation pit.

> Hundreds of people were swarming in the foundation pit, dirt flew
> from their shovels, and the sun blazed on the sharpened metal. . . . The
> wind stirred up whirls of reddish dust. . . and rocked the enormous
> plywood placards with faded slogans reading: "Geiger said: We must!
> The City answered: We will!" "The Great Construction is a blow to the
> non-people!" "The Experiment will overcome the experimenters!"
> (348)

The slogans urging the workers on leave no doubt that this
pit is the same one that Platonov, in his novel, exposed as a
common grave for all mankind, a cruel and illusory foundation
for "socialism." In his preface to *The Foundation Pit,* Joseph
Brodsky declares: "the first thing one should do upon closing
this book would be to rescind the existing world-order and
declare a new age."[15] This is, in a sense, what the Strugatskys
have done: they have used the conventions of science fiction
and/or fantasy to make an imaginative leap out of the existing
world order, and set up an experimental new order in *The
Doomed City.* Nothing has changed, however. History has come
to an end; but for some reason no one has declared the results
of the Experiment. The nightmares that gave birth to a literary
style—broadly speaking, surrealism—in the 1920s and 30s are no
longer nightmares, but commonplace realities. Surrealism is
replaced by Realism.

If we turn once more to the Moscow cafe "The Pearl Oyster,"
we discover the surrealistic premise hidden beneath the realistic
setting. Incongruity appears first of all on the lexical level:

> In our residential massif there is an attractive little eating establish-
> ment. . . (*Doomed City,* 188)

Although the bureaucratic-architectural term *"zhiloi massiv"*
(residential massif) is already so fixed in the language—and
landscape!—that the narrator uses it ostensibly without irony,
the adjective *"simpatichnoe"* (attractive) in such close proximity
is enough to coax to the reader's attention to a sense of irony,
incongruity, and irreality. The words "residential massif" conjure up a geological structure like a primordial mountain range
in which life has long ago petrified into fossil form, or,
inversely, it conjures up one of the conventional science fiction
images of living conditions in a dystopian far future. Here

there can be no question of an "attractive little cafe."[16]   Either
the setting is in the dystopian far future, or the term has no
direct reference to reality, and is simply a bureaucratic cliche:
the narrator uses "residential massif" as a figurative expression
for "housing unit."   The truth is, of course, somewhere in
between the term's literal absurdity and figurative cliche. As in
Platonov's prose, the characters' commonplace reality is shown
to be suspended between absurdity and cliche. The Strugatskys'
use of Platonovian linguistic effects, although not pervasive, is
worth noting for its thematic importance. On Platonov's use of
language, Joseph Brodsky has written that "one can say with
equal veracity that [Platonov] leads the Russian language into a
semantic dead-end, or—more precisely—he discovers the dead-
end philosophy inherent in that language."[17]   There may be
some kind of "linguistic entropy" in Sorokin's Moscow after all.

Beyond Bulgakov

As we have seen, Sorokin's meeting with the bearer of the
trumpet score announcing the Apocalypse takes place in a cafe
called "The Pearl Oyster." If one goes beyond the humorous
and tacky incongruity of naming an urban diner in a continen-
tal city after a marine jewel—seemingly a common practice all
over the world—one can unravel a string of references leading
from the name of the cafe to the Strugatskys' literary and philosophical targets. While the surface plot of the novel can be
understood without these references, the authors have taken
pains to add an extra dimension to the fantastic plot. The
cafe's name is part of a network of references to a prominent
gnostic motif which recurs in several of the Strugatskys' late
novels. The gnostic symbol of the pearl also links the Strugatskys to their most important predecessors in Russian apocalyptic literature; namely, Andrei Bely and Mikhail Bulgakov.
    In the Christian tradition, the pearl appears in the Bible in
the parable of Matthew 13:45 "The kingdom of heaven is like a
merchant in search of fine pearls, who, on finding one pearl of
great value, went and sold all that he had and bought it." This
parable would seem to imply that some would respond to Jesus'
message by giving up everything they have in return for the

greatest gift of all. It is hard to see what the biblical parable has
to do with events which befall the narrator in *A Lame Fate*.
However, there is another source of meaning associated with
the pearl which serves as a subtext to the Strugatskys' work in
more than one instance. That source can be found in the
Gnostic Gospels. The gnostic "heresy" presented the earliest
and most formidable challenge to the establishment of orthodox Christianity and the catholic (universal) canon which eventually prevailed. Although Gnosticism as an alternative religious movement was thoroughly suppressed by the third century A.D., and the texts bearing the gnostic creed went literally
underground, the movement never disappeared completely. In
gnostic teachings, the pearl acquires a complex symbolic significance in a poetic parable known as the *Hymn of the Pearl*. It is
possible to reconstruct the apocryphal subtext to the cafe scene
in Moscow if we consider the context in which the pearl
imagery appears in two other Strugatsky works. There are
echoes of imagery from the *Hymn of the Pearl* in Sorokin's draft
for *The Doomed City*, a novel-within-the novel. Then there is a
whole thesis on the meaning of the pearl oyster in *Burdened
with Evil*, published only two years after *A Lame Fate*.

The *Hymn of the Pearl* belongs to the Acts of the Apostle
Thomas, which is now a part of the Nag Hammadi Codex. The
spectacular find in 1945 of a cache of apocryphal manuscripts
from the first and second centuries written in Coptic (the
ancient language of Egyptian Christianity) did much to reani-
mate discussions of Christ's historical existence and the influen-
tial alternative teachings of His message which flourished for at
least three centuries after His death. In the Soviet Union and
Eastern Europe, scholarly and semi-popularized excerpts and
explications of the gnostic texts enjoyed a considerable vogue.
They were read by an educated public already used to sifting
out the official interpretation and uncovering religious and
political truths between the lines.[18]

The *Hymn of the Pearl* is narrated in the first person by a
prince, who journeys from the east into Egypt, where a great
snoring serpent encircles the single pearl which the prince
must obtain. When the prince reaches Egypt, he adopts the
dress of the local population so as not to be recognized, but

intends to isolate himself in his heart from their "evil ways." Sooner or later, however, he is tricked into partaking of the local food (a symbol, one would assume, of material comforts in general), and he forgets about wooing the serpent to sleep so he can snatch the pearl. When he receives a letter reminding him of his goal, his heart awakens, he remembers the pearl, and is able to hypnotize the serpent long enough to take the pearl and return—in a glorious robe of light, symbolizing inner light—to his homeland. The serpent is Ouroboros, who, in gnostic mythology, represents the evil principle encircling the world. The pearl represents the spiritual essence, or divine principle, from which most human beings have been temporarily separated in their sojourn on earth. The prince encounters many obstacles in his quest, but the notable difference between the gnostic parable and other myths and fairy tales which follow the quest paradigm is that the gnostic prince's greatest obstacle to reaching his goal is not transgressing a taboo, encountering an active agent of ill will, or even death. Rather, in gnostic mythology, the greatest obstacle to reaching the goal is falling into a state of ignorance, forgetfulness, self-satisfaction, and sleep.

The attraction of the gnostic teachings, rather than orthodox Christianity or more foreign systems of worship (such as Hinduism) to Soviet/Russian intellectuals is understandable in this light. Generations of Soviet citizens received no religious upbringing other than an indoctrination *against* religion, the "the opium of the masses," to use Lenin's famous phrase. For many, the texts and teachings of Christianity were no more familiar than any other, and it was natural to draw on a eclectic variety of information to construct one's own spiritual bastion against the secularized and secularizing state. Since at least the time of Stalin, the Soviet professional and skilled middle class has tended to acquiesce to what Vera Dunham called "The Big Deal," in which the Soviet state provided moderate but steady increases in material wealth and social status to those who closed their eyes to the regime's ethical shortcomings. Within the context of the Soviet totalitarian system, then, the sin of willful ignorance, self-satisfied sleep and forgetfulness has arguably been the greatest sin of all. It is no wonder that the

Strugatskys embellish their stories of half-asleep intellectuals with symbols derived from their reading of gnostic mythology.

In the Strugatskys' 1988 novel *Burdened with Evil,* the gnostic parable of the pearl is retold in the language of pseudo-scientific objectivity. The introductory paragraph to this modern-day "Hymn" is, in essence, a popular encyclopedic entry under the heading "pearl oyster":

> In general, the pearl oyster is a rather ordinary and unattractive shell-fish. It is not recommended for use as food outside of dire necessity. There would be no use for it whatsoever, if it were not possible to fashion out of the shell buttons for men's drawers, and if there were not occasionally a pearl inside (inside of the shell, of course, not the drawers). Strictly speaking, there is not much use for the pearls, either, much less than the use one gets from a button, but from time immemorial these white, pink, yellowish, sometimes muted-black little spheres of carbonized calcium have been highly prized as one of the precious gems. (590-591)

Popular scientific jargon easily mixes with bureaucratese and its grammatical offspring—the "objective" passive and reflexive constructions. As far as this species of pearl oyster is concerned, "it is not recommended for use as food outside of dire necessity." The stylistic highlighting of incongruous styles throws a satirical light on the whole passage. More importantly, it refers to the epistemological basis upon which "scientific bureaucratese" can grow: a purely utilitarian, materialist world view. The oyster which is no good for eating or for buttons is considered essentially worthless. The pearl's (jewel's!) formation within the oyster is described in biological terms, like textbook sex, in order to maximize the contrast between the reader's preconceived notion of the pearl's beauty and its natural, almost obscene origins:

> the pearl is formed within the folds of the mollusc's body, in what one might call the most intimate part of its organism. It forms. . . when some kind of disgusting tick-parasite falls into that place. (591)

The language of scientific description is marvelously adequate to describe biological processes, but inadequate to describe spiritual processes. Why, then, have the Strugatskys chosen to rewrite the gnostic Gospels in a pseudo-scientific style?

We can answer the question more fully if we recall that Bulgakov, in *The Master and Margarita,* rewrites the Gospels in the literary language of historical realism. His version of Pontius Pilate's meeting with Yeshua and the latter's crucifixion (in Bulgakov's "realistic" version, "execution") is deliberately set in a human scale, with each character's perception of the moment described in palpable detail. Bulgakov intended to create a version of the Gospels which would strike a modern audience as historically plausible and politically relevant, even as it inverts many of the canonical Gospels' main points. The Strugatskys consciously follow Bulgakov's lead (and Tolstoy's before him), but add an element of parody and stylistic debasement to their anti-Gospel. (For instance, the inclusion of culinary detail in the context of the Gospel story is typical of Bulgakov, and reproduced in negation by the Strugatskys). The choice of a popular scientific style for the retelling rather than Bulgakov's style of historical immediacy is in part due to the Strugatskys' own artistic limitations, but it is also perhaps a measure of what has changed since Bulgakov wrote his apocalyptic novel. Clearly, the Strugatskys intend to mimic the style of Soviet antireligious propaganda, which attempted to explain away religion by giving "objective" accounts of its primitive, mythological origins. Once language is successfully purged of its religious and cultural terminology, though, the perception of spiritual values in human life is endangered. Bulgakov's novel is a powerful vindication of absolute good and evil over the relative truths of history. Any civilization which replaces the realm of God with the realm of Caesar (Bulgakov compares Imperial Rome to Stalinist Russia) is an apocalyptic civilization. The Strugatskys' characters are at least one generation *beyond* Bulgakov's—they are orphans with no spiritual or cultural memory. The difficulty with which the Strugatskys' characters express their intuitions of spiritual values is yet another indication of their location outside of *meaningful* history. For instance, in *The Doomed City,* Izya has great difficulty describing a system of ethical values which give meaning and direction to history without resorting to "religious" terminology.

"The temple [of culture] is not accessible to everyone. . . . The temple has," Izya began to count on his fingers, "well, builders. They are the ones who erect the temple. Then, there are, let's say, m-m-m-m. . . damn, I can't find the word, all this religious terminology keeps creeping in. . . well, ok, let it be: high priests." (*Doomed City*, 478)

In an earlier section we already had occasion to comment on the tremendous difficulty Andrei experiences in trying to formulate an ethical world view using the Russian language as he knows it. His lack of familiarity with Izya's "religious terminology" indicates a lack of familiarity with the cultural landmarks which guide the history (and future) of his civilization.

The Strugatskys' contemporary parable of the pearl dovetails into the subsequent development of Christian culture after Agasfer *cum* St. John's discovery of the gnostic analogy between the pearl and the human spirit. The ambiguity in the date is intentional: historically, both prototypes for the Wandering Jew—the slave Malchus and John the Apostle—were contemporaries of Jesus. John's activity in the "late eighties" refers to the first century, A.D. An analogy with the confusion of faith(s) in the late *nineteen*-eighties is also intended.

Sometime in the late eighties, in the unceasing process of broadening the scope of his titanic metaknowledge, John-Agasfer suddenly discovered that between the bivalve mollusc species *P.margaritafera* and members of the species *homo sapiens* there exists a certain similarity. What in *P.margaritafera* is called a pearl could also be found in people, but then it was called a shadow. Charon ferried the shadows across the Styx. Forever. . . . They were eternal in time, but it was not an enviable immortality, and therefore the value of the shadows as a commodity was equal to zero. Unlike the value of the pearl. (*Burdened*, 591)

By switching from the pearl oyster's common name *zhemchuzhina*, to its Latin species name, *P. margaritafera*, the authors intensify the illusion of scientific objectivity, while at the same time alluding to the intertextual connection with Bulgakov's *The Master and Margarita*.

In her study of gnostic motifs in *The Master and Margarita*, I. L. Galinskaia is able to convincingly point out numerous indications in Bulgakov's text which support her suggestion that Margarita is an incarnation of the gnostic female principle.[19] Galinskaia suggests that Bulgakov was influenced by his reading of the Ukrainian philosopher Skovoroda in the selection of his heroine's name, Margarita. In a single passage, cited by Galinskaia, Skovoroda refers to the feminine origin of the world as the "mother-of-pearl, this margarita" *("perlomater', sego margarita")* (Galinskaia, 88). Bely, too, is aware of the attraction of the Ukrainian philosopher's mystical, anti-empiricist writings to the "eastern" thought of the Russian intelligentsia. In the penultimate line of *Petersburg*, Nikolai Apollonovich "has been seen of late reading the philosopher Skovoroda." It is unlikely that the Strugatskys intended a specific reference to Skovoroda *via* Bulgakov or Bely. It is possible, as I suggested above, that they drew their imagery directly from the famous gnostic parable, the *Hymn of the Pearl*. It would seem, though, that the convergence of their theme with Bulgakov's through the common name—Margarita—indirectly confirms Galinskaia's basic thesis of the gnostic philosophy "hidden" in Bulgakov's novel.

In one interview, Arkady Strugatsky stated: "We would probably have become much more interesting writers, if we could have read Bulgakov earlier" (i.e., presumably before the first official publication in the mid-sixties). This statement supports the view suggested in my analyses of the Strugatskys' role in the development of a Russian tradition of apocalyptic literature beyond Bulgakov and Bely. The Strugatskys' contribution to the shape of the apocalypse in modern Russian literature derives not from an *imitation* of Bulgakov's style and world view, but as a *response* to it.

I have shown how the contemporary, realistic settings of the Strugatskys' novels can be imbued with a metaphysical significance. Sorokin's Moscow apartment and neighborhood cafe are furnished with apocalyptic images. The run-down dormitory in Tashlinsk has apocalyptic graffiti on the kitchen walls. *The Doomed City*, like its geographic double, St. Petersburg (Leningrad), is located between the two metaphysical poles of matter and eternity. The difference between the Strugatskys' apocalyptic settings and those of their predecessors is interesting. In general, in the poetry and prose of the Silver Age writers, as well as in Bulgakov's novel, premonitions of the end of time are reflected in vague and symbolic landscapes of fog, full moon, dramatic sunsets, and so forth. One can refer to these settings as a "meteorological apocalypse."[20]   For instance, the *setting* of 1930s Moscow remains untouched by the supernatural presence of Woland and his retinue.   Only in the final scenes of *The Master and Margarita* does the landscape itself become thoroughly apocalyptic:

> The storm Woland spoke of was already gathering on the horizon. A black cloud rose in the west and cut off half the sun. Then it covered the entire sun. The air grew chilly on the terrace. A little later it turned dark. . . .
>
> The room was rocking with crimson columns. The three ran out through the door together with the smoke, ascended the stone stairway and found themselves in the yard. The builder's cook was sitting on the ground, surrounded by scattered potatoes and several bunches of scallions. The cook's condition was understandable. Three black horses snorted by the shed, quivering and pawing the ground, sending up fountains of earth.[21]

Bulgakov's "realistic" Moscow, darkened by an eclipsed sun and ravaged by the fires of hell, ceases to exist. Apocalyptic events take the protagonists—and the reader—beyond empirical time and space into the purely fantastic layers of the novel.

The uniqueness of the Strugatskys' style is that it erases the distinction between contemporary realistic and apocalyptic settings. On the one hand, the protagonists seem to exist outside of historical time and space: in the Dantean subtext of *The Doomed City,* in the gnostic manuscript of *Burdened with Evil,* and in the fictional subtexts (Akutagawa, Bulgakov) of *A Lame Fate.* Yet, they are also palpably within the Soviet Union in the last decades of the twentieth century. The setting mediates between the fantastic and the realistic layers of the text; it accommodates both simultaneously.

At the end of *A Lame Fate,* the semi-autobiographical narrator indulges in a hallucinatory conversation with his Muse, the author of *The Master and Margarita.* This conversation is instructive, because Sorokin puts his own experience into the voice of Bulgakov's ghost. Sorokin's (and the authors') quest for meaning and value has been redirected by the existentialist reaction to the apocalyptic events of the mid-twentieth century. There has been an erosion of faith in the possibility of transcendence—whether through art or religious salvation. The

Bulgakov resurrected in Sorokin's overly excited mind speaks from the experience of a generation that lived to see Bulgakov's worst foreboding more than fulfilled. According to Bulgakov's Woland, "manuscripts don't burn." Art survives even when the Powers of Darkness rule on earth. That famous statement on the immortality of art is reversed in *A Lame Fate:*

> The dead die forever, Felix Aleksandrovich [Sorokin]. That is just as true as the fact that manuscripts burn to ash. No matter what HE might have said to the contrary. (278)

The fate of the Master (the Artist) is also reconsidered. Whereas Bulgakov's Master earned peace, if not light, as a result of Margarita's interference on his behalf, Sorokin does not earn anything.

> People tend to expect a reward for their labors and their suffering, and in general it is a just expectation, but there is one exception: there is no reward for the suffering of creation. That suffering constitutes its own reward. Therefore, Felix Aleksandrovich, do not expect either light, or peace. You will never know either light, or peace. (281)

It is possible that Felix Aleksandrovich Sorokin is putting the words of his own conscience into the resurrected Mikhail Afanasievich (Bulgakov) who appears at the end of *A Lame Fate.* After all, Sorokin characterizes himself as a successful writer of socialist realist fiction on the "patriotic war theme" who has fully taken advantage of the material benefits his accommodation to the establishment has brought him. Nevertheless, this has not prevented him from also writing a book that reflects the truth. He refers to his book, *The Ugly Swans,* as a "New Apocalypse." In moments of fear and hopelessness, he considers burning his true book, but does not, because "we have hot water heating, no stove." This wane joke reiterates the basic premise of an unfathomable connection between Soviet urban facilities and the outcome of a global spiritual struggle—a struggle which is being waged, for the time being, in the Threshold Cities of Russian literature.

Notes

1. *Grad Obrechennyi* (The Doomed City), in *Arkadii Strugatskii, Boris Strugatskii. Izbrannoe* (Moscow: Moskovskii rabochii, 1990), 483.

2. The Georgian film director Abuladze uses the same horrifying image in his film *Repentance,* when the wife and daughter of a Gulag prisoner search among enormous piles of timber logs for evidence of their loved one.

3. All quotations of Dante's verse are from Dorothy Sayers' translation (Penguin Classics edition, 1986). References are to canto and lines.

4. All citizens of the former Soviet Union carried an internal passport which designated ethnic identity (Georgian, Latvian, Russian, etc.). The Jews were considered the only "problematic" nationality (therefore, Izya's answer is clear) before the Soviet empire and its attempts to ignore ethnic strife collapsed.

5. Joseph Brodsky, "A Guide to a Renamed City," *Less Than One: Selected Essays* (New York: Farrar Straus Giroux, 1986), 69.

6. For a full discussion of the apocalyptic threshold city, see David Bethea's *The Shape of the Apocalypse in Modern Russian Fiction* (Princeton, N.J.: Princeton University Press, 1989).

7. *Khromaia Sud'ba* (A Lame Fate), in *Khromaia Sud'ba. Khishchnye Veshchi Veka* (Moscow: Kniga, 1990), 123.

8. In 1985, the journal *Izobretatel' i ratsionalizator* published a film script the Strugatskys had written called *"Five Spoonfuls of Elixir."* The film script develops the fantastic plot about a secret group of immortals which is not pursued in the novel.

9. In the journal version of *A Lame Fate* (*Neva* 8, 9: 1986), the protagonist is drinking a mineral water recommended for its healthful properties. In the book version, he is drinking wine. In both versions, he complains later that his health no longer permits him to drink or smoke.

10. "Anything you think up. . . already exists. . . ." The narrator's comment paraphrases a statement attributed to Lord Kelvin, and alludes to the Strugatskys' changing views of scientific-technological progress. In a 1970 article (*Literaturnaia gazeta*, Feb. 4 (1970): 5) the authors gave voice to a characteristic disillusionment with the so-called "scientific-

technological revolution" (NTR): "The stunning tempo of this progress has given birth to the conviction that science is omnipotent. . . . and secondly, it has tossed into the arena of intellectual consumption a raw mass of ideas, postulations, and assumptions which could simply be called myths of the modern age, were is not for a kind of ecstatic certainty people harbor that all of this is really possible: thinking machines, non-protein life. . . . "

11. *A Lame Fate.* Version published in *Neva* 8 (1988): 81. It is interesting to note that Sorokin's notebook contains a sketch for *The Doomed City* in the journal version, but in the full book version of *A Lame Fate*, the same passage situates the rainy city of *The Ugly Swans*. This makes obvious sense when the two novels are combined into a frame and inner novel, although, of course, Sorokin could certainly have been working on two different novels "for the drawer," and chosen to reveal only a landscape sketch for *The Doomed City*.

12. Andrei Bely, *Petersburg.* Translated with an introduction and explanatory notes by Robert A. Maguire and John E. Malmstad (Bloomington: Indiana University Press, 1978), xiv.

13. Nikolai Berdiaev, "An Astral Novel: Some Thoughts on Andrei Bely's Petersburg." Translated and reprinted in *The Noise of Change,* ed. Stanley Rabinowitz (Ardis: Ann Arbor, 1986), 202.

14. Andrei Platonov (1899-1951). Platonov's two masterworks, *Chevengur* (1927) and *Kotlovan* (1930) were first published only in the last years of the Soviet Union's existence. Both novels are harrowing visions of a utopian idea which generates its opposite: the decimation of the future generation.

15. Joseph Brodsky, preface to *The Foundation Pit,* in *Platonov: The Collected Works* (Ann Arbor: Ardis, 1978), x.

16. As a matter of fact, in the book edition of *A Lame Fate,* one of the few changes the authors made was to change the word *"simpatichnoe zavedenie"* (attractive establishment) to *"piteinoe zavedenie"* (eating establishment). The ironic incongruity is lost, but the dystopian drabness is made stronger.

17. Brodsky, preface to *The Foundation Pit,* ix.

18. The source of my description of the "Hymn of the Pearl" is a Czech translation and explication by the Czech biblical scholar Petr Pokorny, whose book *Pisen' o Perle* (The Hymn of the Pearl) came out in Prague in 1986. The book quickly sold out at bookstores. The author was praised by intellectuals for having provided them with a sympathetic (i.e., "pro-Gnostic") text, even while trying to toe the then-official party line. For example, on the gnostic view that history is a chaotic, essentially random cycle without Divine, not to mention Marxist, teleology, Pokorny offers a kind of apology: "We must try to

understand [the gnostics] who searched for a haven of spirituality when the world of the Roman empire seemed to be senseless and their path to enlightenment fraught with economic and political barriers" (26). Obviously, in this context the "world of the Roman empire" can be compared to the "world of the Soviet empire" in modern times, and correspondingly, the attraction of certain aspects of gnostic thought today as a "spiritual haven" is relevant.

19. I. L. Galinskaia, *Zagadki izvestnych knig* (Moscow: Nauka, 1986).

20. "Meteorological apocalypse" was suggested by Lev Loseff (personal communication).

21. Mikhail Bulgakov, *The Master and Margarita*. Translated by Mirra Ginsburg (New York: Grove Press, 1967), 370, 377.

Chapter Four

Aliens of Our Time

Gorbachev: *We may differ in our world views, but nevertheless, we are united by a common Fatherland, a common past, and a common future.*
Father Innokenty: *Of course, if you look at it from a historical standpoint. But we christians look forward to something beyond history, and there our futures may be very different indeed.*
—a conversation, 1989

The influence of Nikolai Fyodorov

In the rain-sodden city of *The Ugly Swans,* a race of genetic mutants has appeared, and like the Pied Piper, this race of mutants threatens to lure away the town's children, who are irresistibly attracted to its promise of a better world. On the outside, the mutants—known as "Slimies" *(mokretsi)* appear physically repulsive and sick. They are wet, gloomy, bald, with yellow rings around their eyes—hence, their second unfavorable nickname, "four-eyes." They are housed in a "leprosorium" outside of town. However, they possess a highly developed intellectual culture of their own, and Victor Banev mentions one of the Slimies' own philosophers—Zurzmansor—in the same breath as Spengler, Fromm, Hegel, and Nietzsche.

The Slimies in *The Ugly Swans* represent the same type of supercivilization as the Wanderers (in the future history cycle) or the ludens (in *The Waves Still the Wind*). They dismiss their lesser developed human brothers as one dismisses small children from a meaningful discussion, but they do not concern themselves with destruction or vengeance. They simply select the most promising human specimens to inhabit their utopian space (in this novel, the town's children are selected as the stuff of future humanity) and lure them away from the dystopian present. The Slimies are phenomenally well-read (they seem to need books more than food), and they are asexual. Unlike the Strugatskys' earliest utopian heroes, they have no humanistic illusions, and no moral qualms about their right to select and "save." It is a point worth noting: the transition from the Strugatskys' early science fiction to what may be called their mature prose mirrors a fundamental transition in the mood of their society. It mirrors the rout of humanism and cultural relativism from the vanguard to a weak defensive. It is at this point that the subtextual dialog with Fyodorov begins.

The influence of the ideas of the philosopher Nikolai Fyodorov (1828-1903) on Russian-Soviet literature and science has long been underestimated. The most obvious deterrent to the study of Fyodorov's influence was that his name and his works were taboo for more than thirty years following Stalin's consolidation of power. According to Young, the first mention of Fyodorov in Soviet print after the long silence came in 1964, with the publication of Viktor Shklovsky's memoirs.[1] In the memoirs, Shklovsky reestablishes the fact that Konstantin Tsiolkovsky, the genius of early Soviet space technology, was a student and a disciple of none other than Nikolai Fyodorov.[2] Since then, a steadily growing body of research has begun to trace Fyodorov's diffuse, but far-reaching influence on Russian cultural and intellectual life.

Fyodorov was esteemed as a genius by his contemporaries Dostoevsky, Leo Tolstoy, and Vladimir Solovyov. It was the generations that followed, though, that found direct application in art and in science of the philosopher's grandiose synthesis of religious idealism and scientific empiricism. Fyodorov's maverick Christianity had immense appeal in the turn-of-the-century atmosphere of apocalyptic foreboding and wild millennial expectations. Furthermore, his vision of the concrete, scientifically attainable steps to be taken in the direction of humanity's utopian goal of universal brotherhood remained relevant to the spirit of the times, even after the Revolution. During the early 1920s, the triumph of Marxism still went hand-in-hand with a kind of cosmic romanticism, which envisioned the spread of the new order beyond the boundaries of the state, into the cosmos. Thus, on the one hand, Fyodorov's ideas permeate much of the modernist movement in Russian literature; on the other hand, they provide the impetus behind the scientific research and technological experimentation that would eventually launch the first Soviet satellite into outer space.

The generation of writers who were leaders—or came of age—during the Silver Age were almost all, in some way, indebted to Fyodorov for various aspects of their thought. Mayakovsky's obsession with the motif of eternal life and physical resurrection was fed by his understanding of Fyodorov's thought. Bryusov's "cosmic" poems about life on other planets and his allegorical science fiction stories betray the influence of Fyodorov's philosophical system. Zabolotskys' vision of an intelligent and animated plant and animal kingdom on earth, and humanity's colonization of other planets was clearly formed under the influence of Fyodorov's and Tsiolkovsky's writings. The influence of Fyodorov on Andrei Platonov has received particular attention in recent years.[3] It should not come as a great surprise to us to find aspects of Fyodorov's philosophy given new literary life in the Strugatskys' works, especially once we have recognized their on-going dialog not only with Bulgakov, but with the variety of apocalyptic and millennial motifs which characterized the Russian literary scene until roughly 1930.

However, the chapter in the history of Russian literature which would form a more adequate background to the material presented below has not yet been written—a chapter detailing the decisive influence of Fyodorov's philosophy on the shape and initial development of a native Russian science fiction tradition. Leonid Geller only scratches the surface of this topic in his comprehensive study of the history of Soviet science fiction, before concluding:

> Three main themes stand out disinctly against the background of this fantastic fabric: the transformation of nature over the whole planet, the problem of immortality, and the conquering of the cosmos. These themes were not imported into Soviet literature from the West; they have their source in the philosophical system of Nikolai Fyodorov.[4]

It is not within the scope of this book to fill in the details which Geller leaves out. Instead, we will take a synchronic look at the reappearance of Fyodorovian themes and motifs in the

Strugatskys' work. The complexity and comprehensiveness of Fyodorov's posthumously published writings defies easy explanation and exposition. His philosophy of "supramoralism" is based on the idea that humanity can circumvent the Apocalypse by acting upon Christ's injunction to seek "eternal life." According to Fyodorov, the Apocalypse is not inevitable if humanity follows the right road to God—which is learning to conquer death. Humanity has a clear moral as well as scientific imperative to conquer death, which is the ultimate expression of chaos and entropy, i.e., the opposite of cosmos and harmony. Death is evil, and it is humanity's task to banish death from nature. In order to do so, Fyodorov taught, human beings should stop wasting their time and energy killing each other, and join together in the common task of physically resurrecting our ancestors, as well as achieving immortality for the living. The enormous increase in population brought about by the resurrection of ancestors can be accommodated in outer space, which Fyodorov believed to be the true habitat of *homo sapiens*. In fact, Tsiolkovsky's pioneering work in aeronautic engineering was a direct, practical response to the need for more space for humanity in the immortal future.

A second, related aspect of Fyodorov's thought is that everything in the universe is alive, and that human beings are responsible for shaping and controlling all life by everywhere conquering chaos and death. In other words, Fyodorov extends further a tendency which is already implicit in Eastern Orthodox Christianity; that is, to view all matter as "spirit-bearing" (*duchonosnyi*), and the history of the cosmos as the evolution of matter into spirit. For Fyodorov, the difference which now exists between the life of rocks and the life of human beings is only a difference in degrees of consciousness. It follows that Man, as the highest form of consciousness, is responsible for regulating the rest of nature and guiding it up the path towards existence on a purely spiritual plane. God is relegated to a rather ineffectual transcendence, while Man assumes the central, active role in his own salvation. This "Promethean" aspect of Fyodorov's thought, combined with its emphasis on human transcendence, amounts to a thorough-going rejection of secular humanism. Fyodorov's emphasis is not on the cultivation of the humanistic sciences in the name of gradual social progress; rather, it attempts a synthesis of Eastern Orthodox principles and a rigorous scientific ethos, in order to radically redefine the human condition. Fyodorov's "Philosophy of the Common Task" is based, first of all, on the assumption that death can and should be overcome. Science and technology should be directed towards ensuring physical, individual immortality. Once Man has achieved the means to conquer death, there should be no further need for sexual procreation (since people will be occupied instead with resurrecting the ancestors). This aspect of Fyodorov's thought has much in common with the basic principles of Gnosticism—transformed into literal fact. One version of the Strugatskys' ideological encounter with Fyodorovian Orthodoxy can be found in *The Waves Still the Wind*.

In *The Waves Still the Wind*, the last book of the Strugatskys' future history cycle, a crack-pot scientist elucidates the enigmatic goals and methods of the Wanderers in a document which becomes known as "Bromberg's memorandum." The agenda attributed to the alien Wanderers is based on a crude retelling of Fyodorov's main ideas.

[We] can step out onto the path of evolution of the second degree, the path of planned and controlled evolution, the path to the Monocosm. . . .
The concept of "home" expands to include the whole universe. Man develops a new type of metabolism, and as a result life and health become almost eternal. The age of the individual becomes commensurate with the age of the cosmos—without any side-effects of accumulated psychic exhaustion. An individual of the Monocosm does not have need of creators. He himself is his own creator and consumer of culture. From a drop of water he is not only capable of creating an image of the ocean, he is capable of populating it with animate and intelligent beings. . . .
Each new individual [of the Monocosm] is born out of a process of synthetic art: he is created by the Monocosm's physiologists, geneticists, engineers, psychologists, aestheticians, pedagogs, and philosophers. This process requires several Earth decades, and naturally the Wanderers consider it their most interesting and honorable occupation. Contemporary humanity knows no analog to this great art, except, perhaps, those extremely rare instances in our history of Great Love. CREATE WITHOUT DESTROYING!—that is the Monocosm's slogan. (18-19)

The memorandum contains a point by point exposition of Fyodorov's main principles: the Orthodox vision of a harmonious, altruistic, and spiritual brotherhood of man is to be achieved by the planned and controlled subjugation of nature to the sciences, which will not only overcome death, but also make possible the god-like ability to resurrect, and to create new life. The immortal race will freely inhabit the whole cosmos. The word "monocosm" is an effective Greek calque for the Russian word *sobornost*—a collective wholeness—which is a concept central to Russian Orthodoxy in general, and Fyodorov's interpretation in particular. Furthermore, the jarring juxtaposition, in Bromberg's memorandum, of religious concepts and the language of materialism reads like a travesty of Fyodorov's writing style, which consists of a striking mixture of Old Church Slavonicisms and the latest scientific terminology.

In the evolution of the Strugatskys' poetics, the stature of the hero-as-humanist enlightener (e.g., Don Rumata in *Hard to Be a God*) gradually diminishes, while the prominence of the alien super-human increases. The principle of characterization shifts from the defeat and disillusionment of the enlightener to the power of the Fyodorovian super-human. The shift in emphasis from human to alien is entirely logical and inevitable, since the tangibility of the alien protagonist in the Strugatskys' science fiction grows in direct proportion to the weakening position of the humanist hero.

When one steps back and looks at all of the Strugatskys' works, the pattern becomes clear: the elusive Wanderers of the early future history stories and novels enter the later novels as concrete, developed characterizations, in the form of the "Slimies," the "ludens," and the scientist Vecherovsky in *One Billion Years Before the End of the World* (1976). What all of these characterizations of the Alien have in common is their identification with Fyodorovian and gnostic motifs. The two are often confused: elements of Fyodorov's thought and elements of gnostic mythology often merge into a single system of imagery. Thus, the Strugatskys both record and participate in an interesting process of cultural transformation. Their works reflect the reemergence of subterranean intellectual currents, and the

confusion of various currents, which results in the creation of
new cultural myths.

The Scientists
The Strugatskys' 1976 novella *One Billion Years* is set entirely
within the empirical time and space parameters of a contemporary Leningrad apartment. The protagonist's phone number is
simply Boris Strugatskys' Leningrad phone number with one
digit changed. The reader is meant to feel at home, as it were,
with an ordinary Russian scientist who is pondering a research
problem on a hot July day in the mid-1970s.

The plot begins to accelerate when several scientists in very
different fields are all unaccountably besieged by distractions
and threats which prevent them from continuing their most
promising research. For various reasons, they assume that they
are under attack by an abstractly conceived supercivilization.
This supercivilization defends the principle of "homeostasis" in
the universe by not letting human minds reach too far. By the
end of the novel, there is only one scientist, the mathematician
Vecherovsky, who does not buckle under the opposing pressure
of this supercivilization, be it the hypothetical force of universal
homeostasis or the concrete force of the Soviet secret service
(the novel can be read both ways). Vecherovsky leaves his
unfortunate colleagues and their families behind to go pursue
both his and their research on the top of the Pamir mountains.
The main protagonist Malianov, on the other hand, is a broken
man. Faced with the decision of surrendering to the supercivilization—which appears in the compelling guise of sexual
blackmail, material deprivation, KGB interrogations, and a
threat on the life of Malianov's son—or maintaining his personal integrity as a scientist and as a human being striving for
knowledge, Malianov has no way out. Thus, not only have the
genre's time-space parameters narrowed to the immediate present, but so have the ethical horizons of the main protagonist.

One still detects in Malianov and his friends a trace of the
playful optimism and just-ironic-enough faith in rational social
progress which characterized the scientist heroes of earlier
Strugatsky novels. For instance, in the opening scene of *One
Billion Years*, Malianov is characterized by his approach to sci-

ence as a genuine vocation, rather than a cold profession or dangerous Faustian toy. His playful fascination with theoretical physics is expressed in part as a function of the colloquial, "affectionate" intonational patterns of his language. He addresses the integral he is working on with humorous, half-ironic diminutive forms which are difficult to convey in translation.

> [Malianov] . . . sat down to his paper and pen. Okay, . . . now where did I see that integral? It was such an elegant little integral, symmetrical on all sides . . . where did I see it? It wasn't even a constant, it was really zero! Well, all right, let's leave it in the background for the time being. I hate leaving things in the background, it's so unpleasant, like a tooth with a cavity. . . .
>
> He began to check through yesterday's calculations, and suddenly his heart stopped with delicious anticipation. My god, this is really great . . . Go, Malianov, go! What an ace! Finally, it looks like something is going to work.[5]

However, Malianov's theoretical breakthrough is prevented by a series of frustrating and frightening "coincidences" which prevent him from finishing his work. Several of his colleagues in other fields experience a similar fate. They are soon convinced that they have become the targets of a hostile supercivilization which for some reason wishes to prevent scientific breakthroughs. As they are discussing a defensive strategy over a few bottles of vodka, one of them says, showing off his French, *a la guerre comme a la guerre*. The whole dialog sounds perfectly natural, but it reads double: transliterated into cyrillic letters, *la guerre* becomes *la ger* and spells the Russian word for prison camp. In other words, the "typical" Strugatsky protagonists still eat, drink and crack jokes in between binges of scientific discovery, but the jokes have grown darker, to reflect the main protagonist's new situation as the little man, struggling against overwhelming odds to maintain his sense of freedom and personal integrity in the one area of his life he can almost call his own—scientific research. Ultimately, the State—alias the supercivilization—controls even that.

Gradually, the familiar, contemporary *byt* inhabited by the main protagonist begins to show its surrealistic contours. Another one of Malianov's colleagues, under unfathomable pressures to give up his work, has committed suicide during the night. In an increasingly Kafkaesque chain of events, Malianov suddenly finds himself under interrogation as the prime suspect. After the interrogation, he flees to his neighbor's apartment for comfort.

> Thank God, Phil [Vecherovsky] was at home. As usual, he looked as if he were just about to leave for a reception at the Dutch Embassy in honor of Her Highness, and within five minutes a limo would be there to pick him up. He was wearing an unbelievably gorgeous cream-colored suit, fantastic leather moccasins, and a tie. That tie was what really gave Malianov a complex. He just couldn't understand how someone could work at home in a tie. . . .
> They went into the kitchen [to make coffee]. The whole kitchen began to smell wonderfully of coffee. Malianov settled into his chair more comfortably. Should he tell [about the interrogator's visit], or was it not worth it? In this sparkling clean kitchen filled with a wonderful aroma, where it was cool despite the blinding sun, where everything stood in its place and was of the highest quality—on par with the rest of the world, or even a notch higher—here all the events of the last twenty-four hours seemed even more absurd, crazy, improbable . . . and somehow tainted. (33)

Everything about Vecherovsky's material existence sets him apart from his neighbors and colleagues. His extraordinary standard of living adds to the suspense built into the plot since it functions as an ironic indication that supernatural powers may be involved in the protagonists' plight. The fact that everything associated with Vecherovsky exceeds the normal Soviet standard of living heightens the mysterious aura which surrounds him, as if the exalted status of his clothes and household appliances were the material counterpart (confirmation) of his fantastic personal stature.

Clearly, on the one hand, there is an equation made between a non-Soviet, Western standard of living (it is clear to any Russian reader that "on par with the rest of the world" refers to the developed, Western world) and the superman Vecherovsky, a scientist immune to threats and temptations, who will persist with his own and his colleagues' research. On the other hand, it is precisely in Vecherovsky's material situation, where everything is "of the highest quality—on par with the rest of the world, or even a notch higher," that the normal, empirical world reasserts itself. Outside of Vecherovsky's presence, in the context of everyday Soviet life, Malianov's unwelcome visitors and dead neighbor seem to be part of an unfortunate, but inevitable chain of events. Within Vecherovsky's kitchen, the events which have befallen Malianov seem improbable and absurd. However, what is extraordinary about Vecherovsky is simply on par with the way his Western European or North American counterpart lives and works; it is the discrepancy between this norm and the situation of the Soviet intellectual which leaves room for the surreal and the fantastic to creep in.

The point which must be made is that the figure of the "alien," by the mid-1970s, is no longer an unfathomable cosmic "Wanderer." Rather, he is a human being, a close neighbor and colleague of the scientist-protagonist. Within the surrealistic situation described above, this colleague begins to take on the generic characteristics of an "alien." At one point Malianov notes, "Vecherovsky had an absolutely super-human mind." At another point:

> "Vecherovsky . . . broke into a kind of hollow chortle, which in his case passed for a satisfied chuckle. Wellsian Martians probably laughed the same way Vecherovsky did when they had drunk their fill of human blood. Vecherovsky laughed that way when he liked the poetry he was reading. You would think that the satisfaction he derived from good poetry was purely physiological. . . ." (37)

Both Vecherovsky's intellectual prowess and his personal taste correspond to those attributed to the philosopher Nikolai Fyodorov in all biographical accounts. Fyodorov, who worked in Moscow's leading public library for twenty-five years, was said not only to have known the title and location, but also to have been familiar with the contents of every book in the entire library.[6] His notorious indifference to art and aesthetics has also been noted by all biographers. A few other "incidental" details link the theme of the alien in *One Billion Years* to the Russian philosopher. For instance, Malianov suffers a hallucination, in which his wife's passport shows her patronymic as Fyodorovna instead of Ermolaevna.

Vecherovsky plans to continue his work on top of the Pamir mountains—a location of arch-importance in Fyodorov's understanding of cosmic history:

The center . . . of all the graves of all the ancestors of different tribes is located in the Pamirs; in this, biblical tradition overlaps with the legends of other peoples. Eden, the kingdom of life, was located on the Pamir mountain (today a desert wasteland).[7]

Most importantly, though, Vecherovsky's theory of what is causing the scientists' misfortunes is based on the opposition between the Second Law of Thermodynamics and Fyodorov's notion of humanity's "Common Task." The teleology implicit in this argument holds that the goal of human endeavor is to rise above nature; whereas, to live within nature's laws of chaos and chance is to succumb to unbridled entropy. Malianov recapitulates Vecherovsky's theory in the following passage:

If the law of increasing entropy reigned unopposed, the structure of the universe would dissolve and there would be chaos. On the other hand, if a constantly self-perfecting, omnipotent force of reason gained the upper hand, the homeostatic structure of the universe as it now stands would be disrupted. This is not to say that the universe would be better or worse—it would simply be different. For a constantly developing intelligence can have but one goal: to change the nature of Nature. Accordingly, the essence of the Homeostatic Universe lies in maintaining the balance between the increase in entropy and the development of reason. . . . What is happening to us now is nothing other than the first reaction of the Homeostatic Universe to the threat of humanity becoming a supercivilization. The Universe is defending itself.
   That is approximately it—I don't know if I understood [Vecherovsky's explanation] correctly, or not quite correctly, or completely incorrectly. I didn't even begin to argue with him. Things were shitty enough as it was, and in this light they looked so hopeless, that I simply didn't know what to say, how to react, or why bother to go on living. My God! Malianov, D. A., versus the Homeostatic Universe! (74)

Vecherovsky's theory provides more than an extra-terrestrial *ex machina* which the authors found it necessary to insert in order to solve the mystery and bring the plot to a close. Significantly, in *One Billion Years,* the protagonists are more than willing to accept Vecherovsky's Fyodorovian proposition as the only logical explanation for their plight. Their humanistic faith in scientific progress has proven untenable in a world of "homeostatic" force—and the latter is clearly an allegory for the paralysing lack of separation between Science and State throughout much of the Soviet period. Under these (meta-)

physical circumstances, the perennial Russian fascination with mystical, synthesizing systems of thought is revitalized. The qualities of optimism and faith which characterized the Strugatskys' former humanist hero have been transferred to the figure of the alien. Malianov, who has retained only his humor and his human weakness, cannot help but admire the strength and optimistic audacity of the new Fyodorovian protagonist:

> [Vercherovsky] was going to the Pamirs to struggle with Weingarten's reversals, with Zakhar's work on fadings, and with his own unfathomable mathematics, and so forth. They would be hurling lightening bolts at him, sending him ghosts, and leading frozen mountain climbers, especially female ones, to his doorstep. They would try to bury him with avalanches, they would distort his perceptions of space and time, and in the end they would manage to do him in. Or maybe not. Maybe he will establish the laws governing the occurrence of lightening bolts and mass invasions of frozen female mountain climbers. Or maybe he will just quietly pore over our scribbling and try to discover the point of intersection between the theory of M-cavities [Malianov's research] and the qualitative analysis of American cultural influence on Japan [Glukhov's dissertation]. Most likely it will be a very strange point of intersection, and it's quite possible that in that point he will discover the key to understanding the whole sinister mechanism, and even the key to controlling the mechanism. . . . Whereas I will stay home, meet Bobby and my mother-in-law tomorrow, and we'll all go out and buy bookshelves together. (101-102)

The narrator's slightly hysterical humor notwithstanding, *One Billion Years* is one of Strugatskys' most pessimistic works. The authors find themselves unable to accord to any of the protagonists a glimpse of the way out. The intrepid scientist who will discover the Grand Point of Intersection is at best a Fyodorovian maverick, and at worst a fanatic willing to transgress the bounds of his own humanity. On the other hand, the "human" scientist, family man, and law-abiding Soviet citizen is shown to be pathetically ineffectual in our modern age as it has been characterized by Hannah Arendt: an age dominated by the twin powers of Science and the [totalitarian] State.

Gnosticism and Metaphysical Dualism

We have already encountered gnostic motifs and imagery in the Strugatskys' settings. The radical dualism which divides the world between Good and Evil in all gnostic systems is encoded in the "schizophrenic" landscape—blue-green nothingness on one side, eternal matter on the other. The symbolism of Darkness versus Light; this world versus the transmundane world "beyond," and Matter "burdened with evil" versus the "pure" spirit, is particularly well developed in the Manichaean strain of gnostic thought.[8] (Recall that the Komsomol Andrei in *The Doomed City* is accused of Manichaeism). In the Manichaean division of the world into God's realm (Light) and the Devil's realm (Darkness), the earthly existence we live in, i.e., our material existence, belongs entirely to the realm of the Devil. In the exclusively good realm of God, there are no human beings; there is only pure (non-material) spirit. Thus, to live in a human body is to live with evil, but to live without evil, as pure spirit, is by definition to cease to be a human being. My approach to the study of gnostic motifs and symbolism in the Strugatskys' writing is based on the premise that this seemingly foreign, fantastic metaphysical dualism is not simply used as a science fiction conceit. The Strugatskys are well aware that "Manichaeism" did not arrive in contemporary Soviet society from outer space. Rather, this type of dualistic thought—whatever its origins—has long been an integral part of Russian culture. It crops up today with surprising vividness not only in the popular preoccupation with seances, yoga, faith healing, and other "out-of-body" experiences, but also in serious historical documents written by the country's leading intellectuals. For example, in his documentary novel condemning the Stalinist past, Vasily Grossman writes:

Well, now, isn't it really immaterial whether stool pigeons are guilty or not? So they are to blame, so they are not to blame. So what! The thing that is loathsome, repulsive, is the fact that they exist. The entire animal, vegetable, mineral, physiochemical side of the human being is loathsome, repulsive. Because of that slimy, hairy, lower element of the human essence, stoolies come into being. Stool pigeons are born of human beings. The hot breath of fear of the state breathed upon mankind, and the slumbering seeds swelled and burst open. The state is the soil, the earth. And if the seeds were not hidden within the earth, neither wheat nor weeds would rise from it. The human being has only himself to thank for human dregs.[9]

What is striking about Grossman's statement is its fundamental dualism—evil is an unredeemable, inherent aspect of all corporeal existence. All human, animal, mineral and vegetable life is inevitably guilty and, typically, obscene. The spark of goodness in human life comes from the world beyond, from Man's intimation of the half-forgotten divine essence which was once (according to Gnostic mythology) the pure God. Essential to this notion is an explanation of origins in which the material world is not God's creation at all; rather, it is the work of demiurges.

The significant admixture of eastern, gnostic, dualistic mysticism in Russian secular as well as religious culture surfaced with particular intensity in the first decades of the twentieth century. In part, this was a reaction against the wave of scientific positivism which had dominated intellectual life for most of the nineteenth century. Although the Strugatskys' portrayal of characters belonging to the (male) scientific intelligentsia owes much to the Hemingway-inspired mainstream tradition of western (not "Socialist") realism, their depiction of the Other—women, children, and non-human intelligences,—is inspired by an entirely different, native tradition. In general, it seems that the Strugatskys draw on the imagery of gnostic dualism and "the East" for their characterization of women, children, and aliens. It follows that elements of the anti-empirical, non-mimetic styles of Russian modernist and avant-garde movements in the first decades of this century show through most clearly in the characterization of the Other.

Women

In her study of *The Master and Margerita,* I. L. Galinskaia advances the argument that in the character of Margarita, Bulgakov meant to create a literary incarnation of the theologos Sophia—Solovyov's principle of the Eternal Feminine. Solovyov's Sophia, in turn, is part of the Valentinian tradition of Gnosticism. Briefly, the Valentinian speculation locates the origin of darkness, and thereby of the dualistic rift between matter and [divine] spirit, within the godhead itself. The "divine tragedy," as Jonas calls it, and the necessity for salvation, is a result of original divine error and failure. At some point the pure spirit [God] found part of itself yearning toward creation: "and once this Abyss took thought to project out of himself the beginning of all things, and he sank this project like a seed into the womb of the Silence [feminine] that was with him, and she conceived and brought forth the Mind [*Nous*, male]" (Jonas, 180). The ensuing events, whereby the pure, inconceivable godhead ("Abyss") is separated from its various emanations, who then create the world, is expounded differently in a variety of gnostic systems. The Valentinian speculation presents two symbolic figures, who represent in their fate the divine fall. These are the male Primal Man and the female Thought of God. The latter, usually known as "Sophia," or "Wisdom," is actually made the fallible aspect of God; it is ultimately her passion and her error which lead to the demiurgic activity which creates the world. The ambiguous figure of Sophia, who encompasses the whole range of significations from the most spiritual "Thought of God" to the most sensual passion, is developed in Solovyov's philosophy of the Eternal Feminine. Galinskaia is able to find without difficulty numerous indications in Bulgakov's text which support her suggestion that Margarita is an incarnation of the gnostic female principle, and, more specifically, Solovyov's Sophia. Among these is the observation that in the novel any sexual "relationship of the flesh" between the Master and Margarita is excluded. Once Margarita has taken on the role of the divine Sophia, capable of giving birth to the Word (i.e., enabling the Master to write his novel) her "deceptive incarnation" as a seductive earthly beauty falls away.

With the exception of the female entity of the forest in *The Snail on the Slope*, women occupy minor, subsidiary places in the Strugatskys' novels. Furthermore, the role most often assigned to women characters is either as the victims or the perpetrators of drunken, bestial copulation, performed without love. In *Hard to Be a God*, there is one female protagonist, and she is killed in the violence of a fascist overthrow. In the *The Doomed City*, there are two minor female characters: Selma is a whore, and Mymr is raped by soldiers. In *Burdened with Evil*, the mere idea that the Christ-like protagonist, the teacher G.A., once had a wife and family, seems incongruous to his students. The female figure in the novel, the false prophetess of Islam, Sajah, is portrayed as a whore.

In *The Ugly Swans*, the female protagonist Diana plays an exceptionally large role. Like the one other exceptional portrayal of a woman character (Maia Glumova in *The Waves Still the Wind*) this exception proves the rule: the female protagonist is usually the focal point of a web of allusions to the "Divine Sophia" of gnostic and mystical Orthodox speculation.

In *The Ugly Swans*, Diana is Viktor Banev's mistress. He suspects her of being unfaithful since she is not adverse to participating in the drunken orgies which characterize the social life of the town's bored, cynical, and corrupt adult population. However, Diana is also clandestinely aligned with the dissident forces opposed to the state and the degenerate culture it fosters. She and other dissidents defend the persecuted minority of "Slimies," whose aim is to lead the children out of the corrupt present into a new, super-human future. In the post-apocalyptic scene at the end of the novel, when the old world has been swept away, and the sun shines for the first time in three years on a brand new world, Diana the whore has been metamorphosized into "Diana the Radiant":

> Diana laughed. Victor looked at her and saw that this was yet another Diana, a completely new one, a Diana that had never been before. He had never even thought that such a Diana was possible: Diana the Radiant. Then he shook a finger at himself and thought, "All his is fine, but I'd better not forget to go back."[10]

Thus, the Strugatskys' only thoroughly positive image of a woman appears in the context of a new, other world (hence Viktor's desire to "go back" to the human present), in which Diana the whore is metamorphosized into a divine being. Both Diana and Sophia are names associated with the goddess of wisdom. The Strugatskys' conception of "Diana the Radiant" seems to be at least in part prefigured by the Divine Sophia of gnostic and Solovyovian mythology.

The second exception to the general pattern of female portrayals in the Strugatskys' novels is the character of Maia Glumova in *The Beetle in the Anthill*. Maia is neither a whore, nor a victim of rape, but her relationship with the alien orphan Lev Abalkin involves another, stranger kind of violence. In the following passage, Maia recalls her childhood battles with her schoolmate Abalkin. Unbeknownst to himself (or anyone else), Abalkin is probably a creation of the Wanderers; he is a human agent created by an alien intelligence. Maia recalls her strange schoolfriend's behavior:

> He (Abalkin) beat her—and how! It was enough for her to start acting cocky, and he would hit her one hard. He could care less that she was a little girl and three years younger than he,—she belonged to him, period. She was his thing, his very own thing. She became his thing almost immediately, from the first time that he laid eyes on her. She was five years old, and he was eight. He was running around in circles and shouting out the nursery rhyme he had made up: "The beasts stood outside the door/ they yelled and yelled, but were let in no more." He repeated it ten, twenty times in a row. She thought it was funny, and that's when he first hit her. . . .
>
> It was wonderful being his thing, because he loved her. He never loved anyone or anything else. . . . He had many of his own things. The whole forest around the school was his own big thing. Every bird in that forest, every squirrel, every frog in every ditch. He could order the snakes about, he could begin and end wars between anthills, and he knew how to heal the deer. They all belonged to him, except the old elk named Rex, whom he considered an equal, but then he got into an argument with him and drove him out of the forest. (*Beetle*, 215-216)

One critic tried to interpret this passage as proof that Lev Abalkin represents the Jews—for even as a child he wants to own things![11] The choice of imagery used to depict Abalkin's strange childhood can be better understood in association with a distinct pattern of intertextual allusions.

The forest kingdom, with its elk king "Rex" and incomprehensible natural laws recalls the forest symbolism of Khlebnikov and the poets who consciously drew inspiration from him; in particular Vvedensky and Zabolotsky. In general, for Khlebnikov and the Futurist and absurdist poets, the forest is symbol of the natural world, a kingdom "undefiled by time and death," which embodies an ideal unattainable by man: to merge in harmony and understanding with the mute, inexorable laws of the natural world. The grandiose, mythic quality of this vision is embodied by the figure of the elk in Khlebnikov's poem "Saian".[12]

Zabolotsky's poetry of the 1930s, which in many ways develops Khlebnikov's utopian ideas about the possibility of mathematically understanding and controlling nature, also uses the forest and its community of beasts as a microcosm of the radically new, utopian future. For all its scientific pathos, the imagery of Zabolotsky's poetry is informed by the poet's adherence to the tenets of *Oberiu*, the Russian absurdist movement. His animals and even things are often anthropomorphized, and his poetic world seems strangely pantheistic. The poet Vvedensky, one of the founders of the absurdist *Oberiu* movement, frequently wrote about the rift between his own humanity and the more perfect, timeless harmony the beasts and even inanimate objects share.[13] Finally, an old man in Platonov's "utopian" city of *Chevengur* mourns the destruction of filial relationships in the city (a favorite theme of Fyodorov's) with the verses: "Who will open the doors for me/ Alien birds and beasts?/ Where are you, my parent/ Alas, I don't know![14]

It cannot be claimed that any one of the above texts specifically prefigures the Strugatskys' passage about Lev Abalkin's forest kingdom. However, the striking, archetypical imagery of a mythic forest kingdom controlled by an alien orphan, and the absolute submission of the "fallen woman," cannot be reconciled with the surface plot and imagery of *The Beetle in the Anthill*. Maia Glumova's story in the above passage jars with her characterization elsewhere as a (minor) heroine in the science fiction plot. On the other hand, the childhood scene unites her to the underlying, philosophical theme of the novel, and it carries an echo of the literature which is most pertinent to that theme. It is noteworthy that the school in which Maia and Abalkin fought their battles is called the "Eurasian." Presumably, in the future world of the Strugatskys' future history cycle, geo-political delineations have been radically altered, but Russia still occupies the *cultural* position of the crossroads between Europe and Asia. The modernist Russian literature which loosely prefigures the imagery in Maia's story was a literature obsessed with finding the balance (or synthesis) between the "Asian" and "European" aspects of Russia's destiny, in order to forge for once and for all a new, utopian future.

Male and Female Topographies

But we will leave the forest alone. We won't understand anything in the forest.
Nature fades like night. Let's go to bed. We're very gloomy.
                                             —Alexander Vvedensky

The Snail on the Slope first appeared as two separate short novels in separate years and separate journals. Chapters 2, 4, 7, 8, and 11 of the complete novel were published in the anthology "Ellinskii Sekret" in 1966. Chapters 1, 3, 5, 9, and 10 were published in the Siberian journal "Baikal" two years later. The latter part, in particular, was subject to hostile criticism from ideologically conservative critics. The publication was withdrawn, and for many years versions of *The Snail on the Slope* circulated only in *samizdat* copies. The attack leveled at the Strugatskys by the defenders of Socialist Realism under Brezhnev was essentially banal and predictable, and the significance of the ideological argument for the literary climate of those years has been well analyzed by Darko Suvin.[15] What both critics and fans agreed upon was that the Strugatskys had departed from their straight-forward, adventure style format. The novel was perceived to be more "surreal" than "science fiction," and more Kafka than Bulgakov. One positive reviewer of the English-language edition saw "Kafkian murk . . . joined by Carrollian nonsense." Vice versa, as part of the official campaign against the novel, a reviewer in the Soviet literature journal *Literaturnaia gazeta* in 1969 complained that many readers simply could not understand the Strugatskys' latest work. Unofficial polls circulated by Strugatsky fans among themselves in 1991-2 rank *The Snail on the Slope* as one of the Strugatskys' most successful works. It is also the only Strugatsky novel to have provoked, at least in the West, a well-argued feminist rebuttal.[16]

At the time, it seemed that in *The Snail on the Slope*, the authors abandoned their readable, popular genre format altogether, in favor of a more more difficult symbolic style. In retrospect, the novel appears simply as an exception which proves the rule: stripped of the conventions of detective and adventure fiction (a fast and suspenseful plot), and of the empirical "scientific" ethos (logically motivated dialog and actions, however fantastic the circumstances), the Strugatskys' most experimental novel forwards the dual setting as the most powerful presence in the novel. The schizophrenic setting in *The Snail on the Slope* displays the same principle of composition that we discovered in the novels discussed in previous chapters. Almost all of the cultural and philosophical motifs which were ciphered into the setting of the later novels are already introduced in *The Snail on the Slope* (1966).

The novel interpolates the stories of two protagonists, who never actually meet. Both are intellectuals who mistakenly arrive into the world of the novel from something referred to with longing as "the Mainland." Since the action of the novel takes place in a surrealistic, dystopian world, the Mainland represents, by implication, empirical reality and humanistic culture: a point of reference according to which the protagonists struggle—at first—to orient themselves.

The world depicted in *The Snail on the Slope* is divided into two antagonistic realms: the realm of the Forest, and the realm of the Administration. The Forest is a fantastically fecund, bio-cybernetic entity ruled by females who reproduce partheno-genically. One protagonist, Kandid (Candide) has landed in the Forest. He settles in one of the villages on the edge of the ever-encroaching vegetation of the forest. The villagers foist upon him a child bride named Nava. Kandid takes care of Nava as he would of a young foster daughter. The peaceable villagers are depicted as a primitive culture, although not so much pre-modern as post-civilization: a kind of degenerated culture of essentially honest and quasi-folksy idiots. Proximity to the forest has rendered the villagers almost more vegetable than human: they eat "cheesy" slabs of the ubiquitous moss; they have lost all cultural memory and intellectual acumen. Only the weak resistance they occasionally put up against the "dead-lings," who are sent from the Forest to appropriate more women into its realm, rouses the villagers from a wholly vegetative existence.

The Administration, on the other hand, is a male-dominated bureaucracy devoted to studying and "containing" the Forest. Everyone in the Adminstration is mired in a power structure of rules and red tape which has long since overstepped the boundary of effectiveness and entered the dehumanizing realm of the

Kafkaesque absurd. Here, the deadly organic fecundity of the Forest is matched by the evils of hypertrophic technology and a rigidified, mechanized social structure. Perets (Pepper), the protagonist who finds himself trapped in this realm, is gradually sucked into the mechanism of the Administration, until he himself ends up in the position of its director—a position epitomized by his signature on a self-contradictory and murderous edict to eradicate the Eradicators."

By and large, the hostile Soviet criticism which surrounded the publication of the "Perets" part in 1968 was based on the unspoken assumption that the Administration depicted in the novel was a vicious mock-up of Soviet bureaucracy. The Strugatskys' unfamiliar surrealistic style was probably perceived by many critics as an attempt to divert censors from the underlying anti-Soviet allegory. Western critics also perceived the anti-Stalinist, or anti-totalitarian slant, but rightfully attached a deeper meaning to the forest and Administration imagery than simply a political ruse to get past censorship.

It was possible to see a topical political and ethical theme underlying the conflict of the two imaginary realms: Perets' reaction to an overwhelming power structure could be interpreted as accommodation, whereas Kandid's refusal to capitulate—a heroic but futile gesture which marks him as a kind of "holy fool." Both protagonists try to defend an ethical stance in modern power structures (depicted in the extreme), which have made their ethical principles practically obsolete. Furthermore, one can see Kandid and Perets as representatives of Soviet intellectuals, caught between their fellow countrymen who mistrust them, and their government, which oppresses them. Another aspect of the novel which most critics seemed to have missed is the identification of the forest realm with Nazi-style fascism. In fact, a comparison of Stalinism and Fascism overlays the symmetry of the novel's opposing male and female realms.[17]

In order to make sense of the myriad of contradictory and incomplete interpretations offered above, it is necessary to look more carefully at the extraordinary choice of imagery peculiar to this novel. The question raised by Diana Greene in her article "Male and Female in *The Snail on the Slope*" is pertinent to

our understanding of the work's place in the Strugatskys' oeu-
vre as a whole. Why do the Strugatskys seem to equate the
intellectual's struggle against an authoritarian state with men's
struggle against overpowering women? (Greene, 106) Her article documents the "literal war of the sexes between the patriar-
chal Administration and the matriarchal forest." The two
women who play a role in the male-dominated Administration
"seem more like hostile forces of nature than human beings. In
fact, these two characters approach female stereotypes: Rita
brings to mind the withholding Bitch Goddess and Alevtina
suggests the engulfing mother who wishes to reduce all men to
dependent babies" (Greene, 101). Greene finds that the three
women who rule the forest are not just stereotypes; they
embody the three female archetypes of the virgin, the mother,
and the crone. The forest itself, as geo-biological entity, is
described in terms of a Female—a thoroughly repulsive one.
When Perets makes a reconnaissance visit to the forest, he discovers her revolting cesspools. As Greene points out, the Strugatskys call the cesspool *matka* (womb, uterus), and its offspring
are "whelped" like pups.

> The cesspool was whelping. With impatient, impulsive jerks, she began
> to disgorge stumps of whitish quivering dough onto her flat banks.
> The stumps rolled over the ground, helplessly and blindly, . . . wander-
> ing about and bumping into each other, but all in one direction, along
> a single radius away from the womb into the undergrowth. . . . [18]

Moreover, it is easy for Greene show that "all men in the
novel relate to women in terms of one of three unhealthy patterns: they may try to control women by degrading them, as do
the less sensitive men of the Administration (symbolically, the
Administration builds latrines on the cliff overhanging the forest); they may allow women to prey upon them, forfeiting their
souls, as do Perets and Kvintin; finally, they may renounce
women and avoid sexual relationships altogether, Kandid's
solution (and the one the Strugatskys appear to endorse)."[19] It
remains to be explained why the Strugatskys depict the individual's struggle against the totalitarian state in terms of an
unequal struggle between men and more powerful women.
Furthermore, a paradox arises when we consider the actual

political and social situation of women in the Soviet Union. "In a work exposing the oppression of Soviet society . . . one would, if anything, expect to find women struggling against overpowering men . . . although much has been made of Soviet women's supposed freedom, they have never enjoyed anything like men's personal or political power" (Greene, 106). In other words, the feminist interpretation leads to a paradox: the Strugatskys' gendering of the forces of oppression seems to stand in contradiction to the political reality of women as an oppressed class in the Soviet Union.

The paradox can be resolved, at least in part, when we recognize the forest's specific political referent as Nazi Germany, rather than any one oppressing class in the Soviet Union. There is much evidence in the text which points to concrete analogies between the Administration and Stalinism, and between the forest and fascism. While evidence of the former is fairly obvious, and does not need to be documented in detail here, a few textual examples should help make the latter less obscure. When Kandid, an intellectual from the real world who has been stranded in the realm of the forest, and his native child bride, Nava, make their journey into the heart of the forest, they must spend the first night in a strange village. The village seems "like a theater set"; its inhabitants speak, but have no faces, and the words they speak seem half-familiar, as if Kandid had "heard them in another life." Kandid wakes up in the middle of the night and recognizes the silhouette of a man standing near him: it is his former colleague, a surgeon named Karl Etinghof. He runs after the German into the night, and sees a "long strange building, unlike any other in the forest." From that long structure "a loud cry rang out, piteous and wild, a frank sob of pain that rang in his ears and forced tears to his eyes. . ." Kandid finds himself standing in front of the long building with its square black door, holding Nava in his arms. Karl, the surgeon, is arguing irritably with two women, and Kandid catches the "half-familiar word 'chiasmus'." This word alone, with its connotations of surgical incision and genetic engineering, should be enough to set the scene. The phantom people of this phantom village are all wailing and saying goodbye to each other outside of the building, and Kandid, "since he

was a brave man, and since he knew the meaning of the words
'you must' . . ." makes a move to enter the building with Nava
first. Karl motions them aside. They have escaped—they have
not been included in the death list. They run far away from the
village, and finally spend the rest of the night under a tree in
the forest. When they awake the next morning, the only tangi-
ble evidence of the phantom village's existence is a scalpel Nava
clutches in her hand. None of this is comprehensible to Kandid, who describes the whole episode as a "strange and terrible
dream, and owing to someone's oversight, a scalpel had fallen
out of it." Evidently, the memories of the holocaust which are
part of his (and the readers') experience on the Mainland are
only dimly present now in his subconscious (the reader has no
such excuse).

Even less comprehensible to Kandid (and to the reader) are
the actions of the three women who rule the Forest. The
youngest is a long-legged virgin, the middle one is pregnant—
although evidently without having known a man—and the
oldest, who turns out to be Nava's long-lost mother, insists that
"men are no longer needed." For the forest women, reproduc-
tion is a matter of completely controlled parthenogenesis—but
to what end, and by what criteria is no longer within the realm
of human comprehension. Neither can Kandid comprehend
the elliptic speech of the three women who rule the Forest:

> "obviously insufficient . . . remember, my girl . . . weak jaws, eyes don't
> open all the way . . . surely won't withstand anything and therefore use-
> less, possibly even harmful, like all mistakes . . . have to clean up,
> remove to another place, purge everything here . . ." (66)

The ellipsis dots are part of the text. In its immediate context, the pregnant woman's speech makes no sense. Its only
referent within the immediate context of the story is a fantastic
creature with large horned jaws called the "arm-eater" *(rukoed)*
which is evidently being tortured by the three women. The dislocated sense of *deja vu* is given direction by the key phrases
"weak jaws, eyes don't open all the way," "need to clean
(purge)." Moreover, the fantastic, inhuman forest and its
unfathomable cruelty is linked to the real-life referent of Nazi
Germany by the scene in the phantom village discussed above,

and by Kandid's final, half-intuitive rejection of an ideology that tries to justify the extermination of a race of people on pseudo-scientific grounds:

> but perhaps it's all a matter of terminology, and if I had learned language from the women, it would have all sounded different to me: enemies of progress, drunken idiotic bums . . . Ideals. Magnificent projects . . . the laws of nature. . . . And for the sake of all this half the population is exterminated! (81)

In fact, the Strugatskys have attached all allusions to Nazi Germany and genetic engineering to the biological "Über-Frauen" who rule the female realm of the forest, rather than to the male realm of the Administration. This is still problematic: usually, in the Strugatskys' other works, characters associated with fascist principles are male, and blatantly labeled with Nordic features and/or a German name.[20]

However, there is a native Russian precedent for popular, reactionary, and anti-Semitic cult movements which are explicitly associated with the "feminine" side of the national character. This gendering of national character was advanced in the poetry and philosophy of Russia's pre-Revolutionary, Silver Age culture, as it explored the conflict on every level—spiritual, social, and political—between the "feminine" and "masculine" elements of Russia's identity. In Nikolai Berdyaev's review of Bely's novel *The Silver Dove,* the Russian intelligentsia's ambiguous relationship to the collective spirit of the people, to the Orthodox Church, and to Western models of empirical rationalism is firmly tied to gender archetypes:

> The Russian intelligentsia has always been essentially feminine; its members have been able to perform heroic deeds, to make sacrifices, and to give up their life; but they have never been capable of strong and steadfast activism, they have never had an internal anchor. They have yielded to the elements; they have not been the bearer of Logos. . . . There are some similarities which link the Russian revolutionary and populist of the old order to the Russian decadent and mystic of the new one. Both are under the spell of the feminine popular element, and both are powerless to bring to it the informing principle of Logos. Each is ready to bow before the people—one in the name of revolution, the other in the name of mysticism. . . .
> Bely himself is unable to master the mystical element of Russia through the masculine principle of Logos; he is in the power of the

feminine popular element, he is enticed by it and submits to it. . . . The more [it] lures him, and the more he is drawn to dissolution in the mystical element of Russia with its dark and horrible chaos, the more he worships gnosiology, methodology, scientism, criticism, and so forth. The cult of Matryona [the feminine] and the cult of methodology [bureaucracy] are two sides of the same rupture and disconnection . . . of the elements of consciousness (186, 191).[21]

Berdyaev's formulation and "gendering" of the eternal Russian conflict between "east" and "west," "chaos" and "order" puts the Strugatskys' "surrealistic" descriptions of the dual setting in a new, clearer perspective. The forest is described in feminine archetypical terms:

From this height the forest looked like a luxuriant, dappled foam; like a giant porous sponge covering the whole world; like an animal which was once hiding in ambush, but then fell asleep and grew over with rough moss. It was like a formless mask concealing a face which nobody had ever seen. (*Snail*, 5)

Perets, the intellectual from the Mainland who has landed in the Administration, is strongly lured by the forest's promise of elemental, mystical, "folk" secrets:

"Hot green swamps, skittish trees, mermaids resting on the water under the moon from their secret life in the depths, cautious, incomprehensible natives, empty villages. . . ."

"You must not go there, Perchik," said Kim. . . . For you the forest would be dangerous, because you will be deceived by it."

"Probably," said Perets. "But after all I came all the way here just to see it."

"What do you need its bitter truths for?" said Kim. "What will you do with them? What will you do in the forest? Cry over the dream, which turned into fate? Pray that it could be different? Or perhaps you will attempt the change that, which is, into that, which should be?" (*Snail*, 20)

This forest, with its feminine allure, pagan spirits, and incomprehensible native villagers, is a symbol of the Russian people (as opposed to the intelligentsia) par excellence. Appropriately, it is an Oriental—Kim—who warns the naive, Western-oriented Russian intellectual that he will find nothing but "bitter truths" if he attempts to enter the forest—symbolically, succumb to the populist deception that Russia's future lies in the backward, elemental life of the people. Kandid's experience, in the Forest half of the novel, confirms these bitter truths: the villagers are ignorant, superstitious, impervious to enlightenment, not to speak of democratic ideals. Yet they are neither bad, nor without true faith. It is simply not a faith which the intellectual can share, or export into his own, infinitely more complicated worldview. Kandid learns firsthand the difference between the Russian intellectual's "dream" of world harmony and the villagers "fate." The villagers are ready to dissolve into the dark, all-encompassing womb of the forest precisely because they lack the "masculine" active principle:

> The idea of approaching destruction simply didn't enter their heads. The destruction advanced too slowly, and had begun its advance too long ago. For them, probably, destruction was a concept linked with immediacy, right now, some kind of catastrophe. They could not and would not generalize, they could not and would not think about life beyond their village. There was the village, and there was the forest. The forest was stronger, but it always was and always would be stronger. What kind of destruction is that? It's just life. (*Forest*, 77-8)

The forest, then, is primarily a symbol of what Berdyaev identifies as the reactionary, mystical, sectarian tendencies inherent in the "feminine" character of the Russian people, and only partially a symbol of Nazism. In other words, German fascism is thoroughly "russianized" in the setting of the forest.

Likewise, the Strugatskys' depiction of the bureaucratic Administration which tries to contain the forest owes much more to native Russian literary and philosophical traditions than to Kafka. Berdyaev "predicted" in his 1910 article (above) that the Russian intelligentsia would seek to contain its fatal attraction to mystical populism by hurling its Western "methodology, scientism and criticism" against the people. Thus, on Russian soil, Marxism mutates into Stalinism, and methodology is raised to the level of its opposite—the absurd. The landscape of the Administration is described in terms of masculine archetypes—dry, hard, civilized (urban), mechanical, penetrating:

> The forest wasn't visible from here, but it was there. It was always there, even though you could only see it from the cliff. Everywhere else in the Administration something blocked the view. It was blocked by the cream-colored buildings of the mechanical shops and the four-story

> garage for the office workers' private cars. It was blocked by livestock
> pens of the subsidiary farm, and by the wash hung out by the laundro-
> mat where the centrifugal wringer was constantly out of order. . . . It
> was blocked by cottages with verandas entwined in ivy and crowned by
> television antennas. From here, out of the second-story window, you
> couldn't see the forest because of the high brick wall, not yet com-
> pleted, but already very high—it was going up next to the flat one-story
> building of the Group for Engineering Penetration. The forest was
> only visible from the [overhanging] cliff. (*Snail,* 19)

By now, this landscape is recognizable as the familiar prototype for the landscape in *The Doomed City:* a blue-green void on
one side, and a Yellow Wall on the other; "eternal nothingness
to the left and eternal matter to the right, and it is impossible to
understand these two eternities." Any number of examples
from the text would show that the divided landscape of *The
Snail on the Slope* is a symbolic representation of a divided psy-
che, and of a divided national identity. In the latter respect, the
novel must be seen as an integral part of a literary and philosophical heritage which is particularly compelling to Russian
readers.

Children

There are few child characters in the Strugatskys' science fiction, and they are never depicted as normal or "realistic" children. The most striking traits shared by all the Strugatskys'
child characters are their sexual androgyny, and their otherworldly intellectual precociousness. In *The Ugly Swans,* Banev's
daughter Irma, like all her classmates, has already superseded
her parents' intellectual level:

> Irma left the room, carefully closing the door behind her. She was a
> thin, long-legged girl with a wide mouth and her mother's red lips; she
> smiled politely, like an adult. When she had gone, Victor attacked his
> cigarette. "That's no child," he thought, stunned. "Children don't talk
> like that. It's not even rudeness, it's cruelty, no, not even cruelty—she
> simply doesn't care. You'd think she was proving some theorem to us.
> She made her calculations, completed her analysis, and duly communi-
> cated the results. And then she left, serenely swinging her pigtails."[22]

Irma's unnaturally adult behavior is somehow incongruous with
her little-girl appearance. A list of other children in the Stru-

gatskys' works reveals similar incongruities. The little boy Kir in *The Waves Still the Wind* resembles an androgynous fairy tale "jungle child" more than a "real" little boy. In *One Billion Years Before the End of the World,* one of the protagonist-scientists is saddled with a five-year old illegitimate son he didn't know he had, evidently as part of the supercivilization's strategy to distract him from his work. The boy is uncannily serious and prone to prophetic statements, so that he is treated by the adults with fear, rather than affectionate condescension. The daughter of the "Stalker" in *Roadside Picnic* (1972) is also a mysterious, androgynous creature: her father's exposure to "the Zone" has caused a mutation in her genetic make-up, so that she slowly grows into a golden-furred, inarticulate monkey-like child.

The peculiar traits accorded to the future generation are also well developed in the precocious, ambiguously gendered nephew in one of the Strugatskys' least-known novels, *Hotel 'To the Lost Mountaineer'* (1972). In this short novel, the protagonist is a police officer vacationing in a rustic mountain ski lodge. A few details suffice to make clear that his life at home is utterly routine and devoid of surprising, much less supernatural occurrences. His sojourn in the "Lost Mountaineer" Hotel proves to be full of unusual occurrences which do not easily lend themselves to ordinary legal solutions and conventional law and order morality. The line between the unusual and the truly supernatural remains intentionally ambiguous in order to sustain the tension between the easy solution to the novel's central crime and the more difficult, morally courageous solution. The other guests staying at the hotel provide the first clue that the protagonist has strayed into the realm of the unusual. One of the guests is a famous magician named de Barnstocker, vacationing with his even stranger young nephew.

> The long figure stopped talking, then turned around and faced me. He turned out to have a butterfly tie and exquisitely well-bred features, crowned by an aristocratic nose. That nose could only belong to one person, and the person in front of me could be nobody else but that celebrity. For a second he glanced me over, as if not understanding, then he moved towards me, holding out a slender white hand.
>
> "De Barnstocker," he nearly sang. "At your service."

"Are you really *the* de Barnstocker?" I asked with genuine defer-
ence, shaking his hand.

"The very one, my dear sir, the very one," he replied. "And with
whom do I have the pleasure . . .?"

I introduced myself, but with a feeling of ridiculous shyness not at
all in character with my position as a police officer. After all, it was
perfectly obvious from first sight that the likes of this man could not
fail to hide his real profits, and that his tax forms must be full of foggy
obscurities.

"How lovely!" de Barnstocker sang out all of a sudden, grabbing my
lapel. "Where did you find this? Brune, look, my child, how lovely!"

A dark blue violet had appeared between his fingers. It even began
to smell of violets. I forced myself to applaud, although I don't like
such tricks. The creature in the armchair yawned as widely as its little
mouth would permit and threw one leg over the elbow rest.

"Out of the sleeve," it announced in a hoarse bass. "Pretty weak
trick, uncle."[23]

Throughout the novel, Brune is referred to with a neuter
pronoun. In the context of the Hotel's stylized *fin du siecle*
atmosphere, which deliberately recalls the mixture of cocaine-
laced decadence and triumphant rationalism in Conan Doyle's
Sherlock Holmes stories, the strange child fits in well. However, his presence jars with the very mundane world of Soviet
byt the police-detective protagonist has ostensibly left behind.
An opposition is set up between the ordered, rational,
"western" worldview of the Russian Sherlock Holmes, and the
chaotic, magical, androgynous world of the Hotel's strange
guests.

Finally, there is the hero of *The Kid* (1971) born of human
parents, but raised by a non-humanoid, "intelligent" planet as
unfathomable in its design as Lem's *Solaris*. "The Kid" *(Malysh)*
has adapted to the harsh environment of his planet-parent so
well that his contact with human beings can only end in
tragedy. Here, the question which is always implicitly posed in
the Strugatskys' depiction of otherworldly children is formulated directly by one of the protagonists:

How can one ask such a question: the Kid's future versus the vertical
progress of humanity? There is some kind of logical trick here, like
Zeno's paradox. Or maybe it's not a trick? Maybe one should ask that
question? Humanity, then. . . .[24]

Children invariably represent the future in the Strugatskys
science fiction. They are part of another, alien reality—one that
awaits the present. The future they represent may be a more
perfect, more logical, and more intelligent future, but it is
never a human future. The children's asexuality is just one
indication that the future society they represent is devoid of
human warmth and love, as inevitably as it is devoid of "irony
and pity." In *The Ugly Swans,* Viktor Banev's defense of secular
humanism turns into a plea for irony and pity. He is countered
by the children's Fyodorovian belief in the possibility of
"creation without destroying."

> "Look," said Victor. "You young people probably haven't noticed it,
> but you're cruel. You're cruel out of the best possible motives, but it's
> cruelty just the same. . . . And don't think that you re saying something
> new. To destroy the old world and build up a new one on its bones is
> a very old idea. And never once has it brought the desired results. The
> same thing that calls forth the desire for merciless destruction in the
> old world quickly adapts itself to the process of destruction, to cruelty
> and mercilessness. It becomes essential to this process and always gets
> retained. It becomes master of the new world and, in the final analysis,
> kills the bold destroyers themselves. Irony and pity, my young friends.
> Irony and pity! . . ."
> "I'm afraid you've misunderstood us, Mr. Banev," [the boy] said.
> "We're not cruel at all, and if we are cruel from your point of view,
> then it's only theoretical. After all, we're not intending to destroy your
> old world. We intend to build a new one. It's you that are cruel: you
> can't imagine building the new without destroying the old. And we
> can imagine this very well. We're not destroying anything, only build-
> ing." (*Ugly Swans,* 75-76)

Banev's speech, if it were pronounced in work belonging to
another genre—non-fictional essay or historical novel—would
amount to a thorough-going indictment of both Leninism and
the Revolution itself. It makes no allowances for the possibility
that Lenin's plan to destroy the injustice and cruelty of the old
Russia was good, only to be "perverted" by Stalin's fantastic
sadism and paranoia later on. It even explains why Lenin's
closest co-conspirators in destroying the old world became the
first spectacular victims of the new.

Within the abstract or future chronotope of science fiction,
Banev's speech functions as a prophesy and a warning. While

descriptions of contemporary *byt* and the speeches of "realistic" characters (as opposed to aliens and children) confirm that Marxism has been almost entirely discredited in the Soviet Union, they also indicate that the void is not being filled by a humanistic culture of "irony and pity." Instead, an old and dangerous dream is being revitalized, one that arises in the "eastern" depths of the Russian character. The new "solutions" to the Eurasian empire's problems once again take the popular form of gnostic and nihilistic systems which would ignore the here and now altogether in the name of a more perfect future, from which all chaos and chance will have been banished.

The Wandering Jew

Throughout the Strugatskys' mature work, the juxtaposition between the mundane and the fantastic, the present and the future, the human and the alien functions as a superficial structural device to justify a science fiction plot. On a thematic level, the juxtapostions serve to show that a society in crisis is likely to invent a cruel, inhuman future, regardless of whether it occurs in the name of scientific or religious idealism. If the humanist assumptions (Man is basically good) and tactics (higher standard of living and education) fail to bring about a better world—even with the aid of the twenty-second century's fantastic technology—then a reaction against humanism, and an impatience with history itself, is the inevitable alternative for those who still wish to see some kind of utopian society realized.

As we have seen, women in the Strugatskys' novels usually represent humanity's present regrettable state of enslavement to base instincts. Children and aliens usually represent an alternative, otherworldly, "spiritual" future. Furthermore, even setting and topography can embody the metaphysical polarities which confront—and often paralyse—the "ordinary" hero of the novel. The typical Strugatsky hero derives from the realistic plane of narration, before he stumbles into a world of fantastic subtexts and literary landscapes. This hero is secular by upbringing, humanist by conviction. It can be stated in conclusion that the Strugatskys do not subscribe to the dualistic metaphysics they depict in their novels. The purely spiritual, inhuman future is shown to be ultimately as undesirable as the baseness of the present. The hero-as-secular humanist is put in a position of choosing between two evils, one of which is Absolute Good. In this sense, the Strugatskys are anti-utopian (but not dystopian) writers.

Interestingly enough, in some of the Strugatskys' most complex attempts at welding philosophy with fantasy, a new type of protagonist emerges—one capable of walking the fine line between utopian and anti-utopian solutions. This new protagonist is an updated figuration of the legendary Wandering Jew.

The Legend of the Wandering Jew acquired its definitive outlines in a 1602 pamphlet entitled *Kurze Beschreibung und Erzählung von einem Juden mit Namen Ahasverus*.[25] The *Kurze Beschreibung* gives the story in a nutshell: as Christ was carrying his cross on the way to his crucifixion, he rested for a moment against the Jew's house. The Jew would not let him rest, but told him to keep on walking. Christ answered "I will stand here and rest, but you must walk!" For having insulted Christ, the Wandering Jew was condemned to walk on earth for eternity. The *Kurze Beschreibung* was translated into many languages, including Russian.[26]

The Jew Izya Katsman, along with the Russian Andrei, is one of the two main protagonists of *The Doomed City*. Izya is not the positive embodiment of the "new man" we find leading the way to a twenty-second century "communist" utopia in the Strugatskys' earliest works. Nor does he belong to the ranks of confused and disillusioned intellectuals who populate most of the Strugatskys' novels after *Hard to Be a God* (1964). Least of all does he represent the alien future, characterized by its indifference towards the past, and radical rejection of the present. Izya is an avowed traditionalist, who looks backwards to past culture to find the building blocks of the future.

Izya's spiritual essence does not seek to detach itself from that which is human and lowly. On the contrary, he is literally encrusted in matter ("burdened with evil") since he rarely washes or shaves. Izya fits the classical physical archetype of the Wandering Jew as a gaunt, bearded and disheveled man. At one point Andrei describes him as "terrible, bearded to the chest, hair standing on end and grey with dust, in an unbelievably ratty jacket, through the holes of which one could see his wet, hairy body. The fringe of his trousers barely covered his knees, and his right shoe was torn agape, revealing dirty toes with black broken toenails."(468)

Yet, as Andrei admits with grudging sarcasm, the disheveled wanderer is "the spirit's Leading Light. The High Priest and apostle of the temple of culture" (468).

Izya Katsman alone rises above the material and political illusions Andrei and the City's other doomed citizens live by. In the latter half of the novel, Andrei and Izya leave *The Doomed City* and trek across space and time towards the Anti-city, in a metaphorical journey through the Underworld. As Izya leads Andrei through the desert, he lectures on something he calls the "temple of culture." Against all odds, he is determined to make his own contribution to the temple. The temple of culture, claims Izya, is humanity's monument to the spirit—it is built of noble acts and great works of art. It is built spontaneously and sporadically throughout history by the chosen few, who are capable of giving expression in word, image, or deed to Man's recognition of a part of himself in some transcendent principle:

> I know for certain that the temple is being built, that nothing significant other than the building of this temple occurs in history, and that my life has only one purpose: to protect the temple and increase its riches. Of course, I am not a Homer and not a Pushkin—I won't add a whole brick to the structure. But I am Katsman! And this temple is in me, which means that I am a part of it, and that with the addition of my consciousness the temple has grown by one more human soul. I don't get any of this, Andrei had said. Your explanations are hard to follow, like some kind of religion: temple, soul. . . . Come on, Izya had said, just because it isn't a bottle of Vodka and a double-matress doesn't mean that it is necessarily a religion. (478)

The reader, of course, can recognize what Andrei does not: that there is nothing particularly original in Izya's secular faith in the temple of culture, which he has adopted straight from the Western tradition of secular humanism. However, in Izya the Strugatskys have for the first time divorced the Western ideal of secular humanism from the "eastern" longing for utopia. The Ideal is housed in the crass, unheroic body of one of earth's survivors; it no longer belongs to the characterization of the "new man." Izya is not an optimistic twenty-second century Progressor spreading the word to backward planets; nor is he an agent of the "Wanderers," the "Ludens," or the "Slimies." Although he fulfills the same role as these otherworldly "pipers" by luring Andrei away from the material comfort, boredom, and spiritual emptiness of the majority, he does not lead him off into a non-human future, whether good or bad. Izya is eternally human, for as an incarnation of the Wandering Jew, he is eternally on this earth, as, typically, his concern with ecology, rather than technology, would indicate: "[I have three daughters], but not one of them knows what Siberian salmon tastes like. I explained to them about salmon, sturgeon—extinct species,—and someday they'll tell their children the same about herring"(476).

In his comprehensive study of the Wandering Jew archetype, G. K. Anderson assesses the Wanderer's new role in the twentieth century:

> Eternal wandering is the ultimate punishment in many mythologies. Blasphemy comes from overweening pride, and by that sin fell the angels. And when the moderns inherited the Legend, their message seemed to be: *Ecce Homo!* Behold the man who sinned and is being punished for it amid all these terrors; but look again, see how he represents the spirit of revolt, of unconquered courage, of the very Jewish race itself; and "what else is not to be overcome." (Anderson, 10)

Izya has built a cairn of stones in the desert wilderness and buried within it his manuscript "A Guide to a Delirious World" which describes the path from the end of history (in Izya's version, the end begins with Chernyshevsky's "Crystal Palace," which represents total material abundance for all) to the end of the world (true spiritual enlightenment). Andrei's initial uncomprehending condemnation of Izya's temple of culture turns to admiration by the final stage of their journey together:

> No, [Andrei] thought, everything is correct and as it should be: no normal person will ever reach this cairn. A normal person, when he reaches the Crystal Palace, will stay there for the rest of his life. I saw them there—normal people. Let me tell you, if someone gets as far as this cairn, it will be some kind of Izya-Number-Two. When he breaks down this cairn and opens the manuscript he'll immediately forget

about everything else. He'll die here, reading. . . . Although, on the
other hand, how did I get this far? (476)

Izya is the earliest incarnation of the Wandering Jew to
appear in the Strugatskys' work, and his presence indicates that
the authors had set themselves a new artistic task (continued in
their later work, *Burdened with Evil).* From now on, they would
not so much search for the "new man" of the future, as for the
enduring qualities in the "old" humanity which allow a few to
"get this far."

Notes

1. George Young, *Nikolai Fedorov: An Introduction* (Belmont, Mass.: Norland Publishing Company, 1979).

2. Konstantin Tsiolkovsky (1857–1935) laid the theoretical and practical groundwork for modern space technology in the Soviet Union. An excellent short essay on the relationship between Tsiolkovsky and Fyodorov is Michael Holquist's "The Philosophical Bases of Soviet Space Exploration," *The Key Reporter*, vol. 51, No. 2, Winter 1985-6 (Wash., D.C.: Phi Beta Kappa Society).

3. Valery Bryusov (1873–1924), poet, novelist, and critic, was a leader of the Russian Symbolist movement at the beginning of the century. Vladimir Mayakovsky (1893–1930), one of the most prominent Russian poets of the twentieth century, contributed his overwhelming stature and talent both to the pre-Revolutionary Futurist movement in the arts and to the new propagandistic art after the Revolution. Nikolai Zabolotsky (1903–1958), poet. The yearning for individual immortality is a theme which runs throughout his poetry. For Fyodorov's influence on Platonov, see Ayleen Teskey, *Platonov and Fyodorov: The Influence of Christian Philosophy on a Soviet Writer* (England: Avery Publishing Company, 1982).

4. Leonid Geller. *Vselennaia za predelom dogmy* (London: Overseas Publications, 1985), 63.

5. *Za milliard let do kontsa sveta* (One Billion Years Before the End of the World), in *Arkadii Strugatskii, Boris Strugatskii. Izbrannoe.* (Moscow: Moskovskii rabochii, 1990), 5.

6. Young, 11.

7. Nikolai Fedorov, *Filosofia obshchego delo*, ed. Peterson. Vol. 1 (England: Gregg International Publishers, 1970), 247.

8. See Hans Jonas, *The Gnostic Religion*, 2nd ed. (Boston: Beacon Press, 1963), and Samuel Lieu, *Manichaeism* (Manchester and Dover, N.H.: Manchester University Press, 1985).

9. Vasily Grossman, *Forever Flowing* (Stanford: Hoover Institution Press, 1990), 82. The translation is by Thomas P. Whitney.

10. *The Ugly Swans*, trans. Alice Stone Nakhimovsky and Alexander Nakhimovsky (New York: Macmillan, 1979), 234. All quotations are from the

excellent Nakhimovsky translation. The first Russian publication of *Gadkie lebedi* (The Ugly Swans) was an unauthorized edition which came out in the West in 1972. The novel was not officially published in the Soviet Union until 1987, under the title *Vremia Dozhdia* (A Time of Rain). In the latest editions of the Strugatskys' works, the text of *The Ugly Swans* is published according to the authors original conception: as part of the novel *A Lame Fate*.

11. This unconvincing argument was put forth by Maia Kaganskaia in a stunningly far-fetched, but entertaining article, "Rokovye Iaitsa: Razdum'ia o nauchnoi fantastike voobshche i brat'ev Strugatskykh v osobennosti," *Dvadtsat' Dva*, Nos. 43, 44, 55 (1985 and 1987).

12. Velemir Khlebnikov (1885–1922). One of the leaders of the Russian cubo-futurists, his highly original artistic output ranges over a kind of primitivism, cosmic mythology, primordial Slavic utopianism, transsense verbal experiments, and a conviction that magic inheres in language. He was a great source of inspiration to linguists as well as to avant-garde artists.

13. *Oberiu* (Ob'edinenie real'nogo iskusstva, "Association for Real Art") was an avantgard literary group active in Leningrad from 1927 to 1930. See also Alice Stone Nakhimovsky, *Laughter in the Void. An Introduction to the Writings of Daniil Kharms and Alexander Vvedenskii* (Vienna: Wiener Slawistischer Almanach, Sonderband 5, 1982).

14. Andrei Platonov. *Chevengur* (Paris: YMCA Press, 1972), 244. In Russian, Platonov's verses are very similar to the strange refrain Abalkin repeats. Abalkin's lines are *"stoiali zveri okolo dveri, oni krichali, ikh ne puskali;"* in *Chevengur* we find *"kto otopret mne dveri, chuzhie ptitsi, zveri? I gde ty, moi roditel', uvy, ne znaiu ia"*.

15. See Darko Suvin, "Criticism of the Strugatsky Brothers' Work," *Canadian-American Slavic Studies* 2 (Summer 1972), 286 307.

16. See Diana Greene, "Male and Female in *The Snail on the Slope*," *Modern Fiction Studies*, vol. 2, no.1 (Spring 1986): 97 107.

17. See Darko Suvin's introduction to the English language edition of *The Snail on the Slope* (Bantam Books, 1980), 1-20. For other viewpoints, I am indebted to Konstantin Kustanovich, whose unpublished Master's thesis (Columbia University) treats this novel, and to Omry Ronen, whose strenuous objection to superficial interpretations revealed better ones underneath.

18. *Les* (Ann Arbor: Ardis, 1981), 83 84. My citations are from the Russian language editions printed in the West. The Ardis version contains the Kandid chapters only, hence the title "The Forest." The Possev publication with the title *The Snail on the Slope* contains the Perets chapters only. My citations refer to the Possev edition: *Ulitka na sklone* (Frankfurt/Main: Possev Verlag, 1972). The existing English language

translation (Bantum Books, 1980) contains both halves. The Strugatskys' original version of the novel is now being reissued and printed in its entirety by post-glasnost presses.

19. Greene, 105.

20. Fritz Geiger is the Hitler-esque dictator in *The Doomed City,* and Marek Parasuxin, despite his very Russian name, is distinguished by his blond, Nordic features and his black leather SS jacket in *Burdened with Evil.*

21. From Berdyaev's essay "Russkii soblazn': po povodu *Serebr'anogo golubia A. Belogo.*" Originally printed in *Russkaia Mysl'* 11: 1910. Page numbers refer to Stanley Rabinowitz's translation in *The Noise of Change* (Ann Arbor: Ardis, 1986), 185 195.

22. Translated by Nakhimovsky and Nakhimovsky, *The Ugly Swans,* 1.

23. *Otel' 'U pogibshego al'pinista'* (Hotel "To the Lost Moutaineer"), (Moscow: Detskaia Literatura,1983), 13.

24. *Malysh* (The Kid), (Melbourn, Australia: Izdatel'stvo Artol, 1985), 140.

25. See George Anderson, *The Legend of the Wandering Jew.* I am much indebted to Anderson's comprehensive study for the general outlines of the legend.

26. The best bibliographical aid to the legend of the Wandering Jew on Slavic territory is Avrahm Yarmolinsky, "The Wandering Jew," *Studies in Jewish Bibliography and Related Subjects* (New York, 1929).

Conclusion

A Postscript on Science in the Strugatskys' Science Fiction

In the previous chapters, I singled out the Strugatskys' apocalyptic motif and elaborated upon the way in which they use some of the conventions of the science fiction genre to actually create a double exposure of two narrative planes: 1. the realistic depiction of a contemporary society in crisis; and 2. the fantastic depiction of that society's myths about the origins, significance, and solutions to the crisis. It has been made abundantly clear that "apocalyptic realism" does not rely on the hard sciences and technology for its imagery, or to motivate the plot. The role of science in the Strugatskys' fiction is at once more subtle, and more profound. The paradigms of science, as much as the paradigms of religion and the arts, have a powerful prefigurative presence in all of the Strugatskys' writing. The development of science, the dynamics of scientific communities, the "way science was done" in the former Soviet Union, and the phenomenon of "Strugatskyism" (i.e., avid fan readership) among the Russian scientific and technical intelligentsia—these areas are intricately related and open to study from an interdisciplinary point of view. One consideration is the recent history of changing areas of focus, or dominant research trends, in the fields of physics, mathematics, genetics, neurobiology, and so forth. Another consideration is the Strugatskys' personal and professional connections over the last four decades with working Russian scientists. A third consideration is the way in which the Strugatskys' awareness of, and reaction to, shifting scientific paradigms is reflected in their fiction.

In the last chapter, we found that the Strugatskys' "new man" is gradually displaced by two symbolic figures: the unfathomable alien, who symbolizes the unrealistic and dangerous utopian assumptions behind the notion of a perfectible society; and the Wandering Jew, who symbolizes the ability to endure without illusions. Furthermore, the optimistic scientists who take over an institute of parapsychology in *Monday Begins on Saturday* (1965) are left fighting a hopeless battle with powers beyond their control in *One Billion Years* (1976). One should recall that the Soviet "new man" was not only an obligatory builder of socialism in Socialist Realist fiction and propaganda, he (and she) was also, in the 1960s, a positive new type of educated citizen with genuine hopes for the wedding of science (particularly cybernetics) and social progress. The Strugatskys' most popular early novel, *Monday Begins on Saturday*, depicted the "new men" of their generation at work: enthusiastic young scientists defying both the backwardness of their technology and the rigidity of Soviet bureaucracy with marvelous results. The novel was a *tour de force* of comic sociological modeling and a veritable *commedia dell'arte* of existing scientific research community structures.

It seems to me now that the marked change in style and tone in the Strugatskys' later works also reflects a change in the dynamics of the *scientific communities* the Strugatskys model. I have not pursued that line of inquiry here, because it represents a sequel to this study, as well as a fitting conclusion. The collapse of the Soviet Union has prompted an exodus of scientific talent from Russia to the West. Thus, the remaining scientists, who have neither left the country, nor their vocation, find themselves without funds and equipment (which the State can no longer afford), without colleagues, and without the generational continuity which ensures that the scientific tradition of a given society is passed on. Much has already been made in scientific and government circles, both East and West, of the "apocalyptic" situation of the scientific community in Russia. The negative aspects of the "brain drain" are balanced by hopes for productive collaboration of a truly internationalized scientific community. In any case, it seems likely that the Strugatskys' science fiction will gain new relevance as science history—as a portrait of the intellectual, inter-personal, political, linguistic, and mundane concerns which formed the fabric of scientific culture in the Soviet Union.

Appendix

Chronological Overview of the Strugatskys' Prose Fiction

The most comprehensive listing of all stories, books, plays, articles, film scripts and critical works by the Strugatskys is privately distributed by the "Ludens," a small group of Strugatsky disciples who share among themselves a lap-top publication called *"Ponedelniki"* (Mondays). The Russian publishing cooperative "Tekst" [125190 Moscow, A-190, a/ya 89] is compiling a full bibliographical reference source on the Strugatskys (date to press unknown).

For a chronological overview, the Strugatskys' novels and novellas are listed below according to the earliest year of publication in the Soviet Union. With a few exceptions, all of these works have been reprinted and anthologized numerous times, by different branches of the Soviet publishing enterprise.

1959. *Strana bagrovykh tuch* (Land of the Crimson Clouds)

1960. *Put' na Amal'teiu* (Journey to Amalthea)

1962. *Stazheri* (The Apprentices)

1962. *Popytka k begstvu* (Escape Attempt)

1962. *Polden': 22 vek* (Noon: 22nd Century), revised, expanded and reprinted in 1967.

1963. *Dalekaia Raduga* (Far Rainbow)

1964. *Trudno byt' bogom* (Hard to Be a God)

1965. *Ponedel'nik nachinaetsia v subbotu* (Monday Begins on Saturday)

1965. *Khishchnye veshchi veka* (Predatory Things of our Time)

1966. *Ulitka na sklone* (The Snail on the Slope), "Kandid" chapters only. Subsequently withdrawn from publication.

1967. *Vtoroe Nashestvie Marsian* (The Second Invasion From Mars)
Subsequently withdrawn from publication.

1968. *Ulitka na sklone* (The Snail on the Slope), "Perets" chapters only. Subsequently withdrawn from publication.

1968. *Skazka o troike* (Tale of the Troika)
Subsequently withdrawn from publication.

1969. *Obitaemyi ostrov* (The Inhabited Island)

1970. *Otel' "U pogibshego al'pinista* (Hotel "To the Lost Mountaineer")

1971. *Malysh* (The Kid)

1972. *Piknik na obochine* (Roadside Picnic)

1974. *Paren' iz preispodnei* (The Guy From Hell)

1976. *Za milliard let do kontsa sveta* (One Billion Years Before the End of the World)

1979. *Zhuk v muraveinike* (The Beetle in the Anthill)

1985. *Volni gasiat veter* (The Waves Still the Wind)

1986. *Khromaia Sud ba* (A Lame Fate). Portions of this novel were written in the early 70s, and include the text of *The Ugly Swans* within the frame novel.

1987. *Gadkie Lebedi* (The Ugly Swans). Written in the early 1970s and published in the West in 1972 (Germany) and 1979 (English translation).

1988. *Grad Obrechennyi* (The Doomed City). Written in the mid-70s.

1988. *Otiagoshchennye zlom, ili sorok let spustia* (Burdened with Evil, or Forty Years Later)

Selected Bibliography

1. Works by Arkady and Boris Strugatsky

Russian editions cited in the main text, in chronological order of original date of publication.

Les (The Forest). Ann Arbor: Ardis, 1981. Contains the "Kandid" chapters of *The Snail on the Slope*.

Ulitka na sklone (The Snail on the Slope). Frankfurt/Main: Possev Verlag, 1972. Contains the "Perets" chapters only.

Otel' 'U pogibshego al'pinista' (Hotel "To the Lost Mountaineer"). Moscow: Detskaia Literatura, 1983.

Malysh (The Kid). Melbourn, Australia: Izdatel'stvo Artol, 1985.

Za milliard let do kontsa sveta (One Billion Years Before the End of the World). In *Arkadii Strugatskii, Boris Strugatskii. Izbrannoe*, 3-102. Moscow: Moskovskii rabochii, 1990.

Zhuk v muraveinike (The Beetle in the Anthill). In *Zhuk v muraveinike: rasskazy i povesti*. Riga: Liemsa, 1986.

Volni gasiat veter (The Waves Still the Wind). Haifa, Israel: N.p., 1986.

Khromaia Sud'ba (A Lame Fate). In *Khromaia Sud'ba. Khishchnye Veshchi Veka*, 3-283. Moscow: Kniga, 1990.

Grad Obrechennyi (The Doomed City). In *Arkadii Strugatskii, Boris Strugatskii. Izbrannoe*, 169-483. Moscow: Moskovskii rabochii, 1900.

Otiagoshchennye zlom, ili sorok let spustia (Burdened with Evil, or Forty Years Later). In *Arkadii Strugatskii, Boris Strugatskii. Izbrannoe*, 484-639. Moscow: Moskovskii rabochii, 1900.

Zhidy goroda Pitera, ili neveselye besedy pri svechax. Komedia v dvukh deistviiakh (Yids of the City of Peter, or gloomy discussions by candlelight. A comedy in two acts). *Neva* 9 (1990): 92-115.

2. English Translations of the Strugatskys' Works

The following titles were published in hardback in Macmillan's "Best of Soviet Science Fiction Series" (New York: Macmillan Publishing Co., Inc.) and reprinted in paperback in the Collier Books Edition (New York: Collier Books). The quality of translation is generally good.

Roadside Picnic/Tale of the Troika. Macmillan, 1977. *Roadside Picnic* was also published in paperback by Penguin Books, 1982.

Prisoners of Power. Macmillan, 1977; Collier, 1978. This is a translation of *The Inhabited Island.*

Definitely Maybe. Macmillan, 1978; Collier, 1978. This is a translation of *One Billion Years Before the End of the World.*

Noon: 22nd Century. Macmillan, 1977; Collier, 1979.

Far Rainbow/The Second Invasion from Mars. Macmillan, 1979; Collier, 1980.

Beetle in an Anthill. Macmillan, 1980.

Escape Attempt. Macmillan, 1982.

The Ugly Swans. Macmillan, 1979; Collier, 1980.

Outside of the Macmillan series, the following novels have been published in English.

Hard to Be a God. New York: DAW Books, Inc., 1973.

Monday Begins on Saturday. New York: DAW Books, Inc., 1977. This is an inadequate translation of one of the Strugatskys' greatest hits, but it is still readable.

The Final Circle of Paradise. New York: DAW Books, Inc., 1976. This is a translation of *Predatory Things of our Time*.

The Snail on the Slope. New York: Bantam Books, 1980. This edition includes an informative introduction by Darko Suvin.

The Time Wanderers. New York: St. Martin's Press, 1986. This is an extremely poor translation of *The Waves Still the Wind*.

3. Books, articles, interviews

Adorno, T. "Freudian Theory and the Pattern of Fascist Propaganda." In *The Essential Frankfurt Reader*, eds. Arato and Gebhardt, 118-137. New York, 1987.

Alewyn, R. "Das Ratsel des Detektivromans." In *Definitionen: Essays zur Literatur*, 117-136. Frankfurt/Main, 1963.

Amusin, M. "Daleko li do budushchego?" *Neva* 34, no. 2 (1988): 153-160.

Anderson, G. *The Legend of the Wandering Jew*. Providence: Brown University Press, 1965.

Arendt, H. *On Revolution*. New York: Viking, 1963.

Auerbach, E. *"Figura"* in the Phenomenal Prophecy of the Church Fathers." In *Scenes from the Drama of European Literature*. New York, 1959.

Bartol'd, V. V. "Museilima." In *Sochineniia. Raboty po istorii islama i arabskogo khalifata*. Vol. 6. Moscow: Akademiia Nauk (1966): 549-574.

Bailes, K. "Science, Philosophy and Politics in Soviet History: The Case of Nikolai Vernadskii." *Russian Review* 40, no. 3 (July 1981): 278-299.

Berdiaev, Nikolai. *Russkaia Ideia.* Paris: YMCA Press, 1946. Translated as *The Russian Idea.* New York: Macmillan, 1948.

Berdiaev, Nikolai. "An Astral Novel: some Thoughts on Andrei Bely's *Petersburg.*" In *The Noise of Change.* Translated and edited by Stanley Rabinowitz. Ann Arbor: Ardis, 1986.

Bethea, D. *The Shape of the Apocalypse in Modern Russian Fiction.* Princeton: Princeton University Press, 1989.

Bloch, E. *The Utopian Function of Art and Literature: Selected essays.* Translated by Jack Zipes and Frank Mecklenburg. Cambridge: MIT Press, 1988.

Bocharov, A. *Literatura i vremia: iz tvorcheskogo opyta prozy 60x-80x godov.* Moscow, 1988.

Britikov, A. F. "Detektivnaia povest" v kontekste prikliuchenet-skikh zhanrov" In *Russkaia-sovietskaia povest' 20x-30x godov.* Leningrad, 1976.

——. *Russkii-sovietskii nauchno-fantasticheskii roman.* Leningrad, 1970.

Browning, R. *The Complete Works of Robert Browning.* Vol. 3. Ohio University Press, 1971.

Cioran, S. *Vladimir Soloviev and the Knighthood of the Divine Sophia.* Canada: Wilfred Laurier University Press, 1977.

Court, J. *Myth and History in the Book of Revelation.* Atlanta: John Knox Press, 1979.

Csicsery-Ronay, I. "Towards the Last Fairy Tale: On the Fairy Tale Paradigm in the Strugatskys' Science Fiction, 1963-72." *Science Fiction Studies* 13 (1986): 1-41.

Dunham, Vera. *In Stalin's Time: Middleclass Values in Soviet Fiction.* Cambridge [Eng.]; New York: Cambridge University Press, 1976.

Dodds, E. R. "On Misunderstanding Oedipus." *Greece and Rome* 13, 1966.

Eickelman, D. "Musaylima: An Approach to the Social Anthropology of Seventh-Century Arabia." *Journal of the Economic and Social History of the Orient* 10 (July, 1967): 17-52.

Fedorov, N. *Filosofia Obshchego Dela.* Edited by Peterson. 2 vols. England: Gregg International Publishers, 1970.

Frolov, A. F. "Nauchno-fantastiheskoe proizvedenie i ego chitatel': povest' A. i B. Strugatskikh Za milliard let do kontsasveta." *Problema zhanra.* Dushanbe, 1984.

Fisch, H. *A Remembered Future.* Bloomington: Indiana University Press, 1984.

Galinskaia, I. L. *Zagadki izvestnykh knig.* Moscow: Nauka, 1986.

Geller, L. *Vselennaia za predelom dogmy.* London: Overseas Publications Interchange Ltd., 1985.

Graham, L. *Science, Philosophy and Human Behavior in the Soviet Union.* New York: Columbia University Press, 1987.

Greene, D. "Male and Female in *The Snail on the Slope* by the Strugatsky Brothers." *Modern Fiction Studies* 32, no. 1 (Spring 1986): 97-107.

Heissenbuttel, H. "Spielregeln des Kriminalromans." In *Trivialliteratur,* 162-175. Berlin: Schmidt-Henkel, 1964.

Holquist, M. "The Philosophical Bases of Soviet Space Exploration" In *The Key Reporter* 51, no. 2 (Winter 1985-6).

Jameson, F. "Generic Discontinuities in Science Fiction: Brian Aldiss' *Starship.*" *Science Fiction Studies* 1: 1973.

Jonas, H. *The Gnostic Religion.* Sd ed. Boston: Beacon Press, 1963.

Kaganskaia, M. "Rokovye iaitsa (Razdum'ia o nauchno-fantastike voobshche i brat'iakh Strugatskikh v osobennosti)" *Dvadtsat' Dva* 43, 44, 55, 1985-7.

Kanchukov, E. "Detstvo v proze Strugatskikh" *Detskaia Literatura* 57, no. 3 (1988): 29-33.

Lapunov, B. *V mire fantastiki*. Moscow, 1975

Lieu, S. N. C. *Manichaeism in the later Roman Empire and Medieval China: a historical survey*. Manchester and Dover, N.H.: Manchester University Press, 1985.

Lotman, Iu. M. and Uspenskii, B. A. "Binary Models in the Dynamics of Russian Culture." In *The Semiotics of Russian Cultural History*. Edited by Alexander and Alice Nakhimovsky, 30-66. Ithaca and London: Cornell University Press, 1985.

Lemkhin, M. "Tri povesti brat'ev Strugatskikh" *Grani* 139 (1986): 93-117.

Manuel, F.E., and Manuel, F.P. *Utopian Thought in the Western World*. Cambridge, Mass.: Belknap Press, 1979.

Marsch, E. *Die Kriminalerzahlung: Theorie, Geschichte, Analyse*. Munich, 1972.

Masing-Delic, I. "Zhivago as a Fedorovian Soldier" *Russian Review* 40, no. 3 (July 1981): 300 316.

McGuire, P. "Future History, Soviet Style: The Work of the Strugatsky Brothers" In *Critical Encounters*. Edited by Tom Staicar. New York, 1982.

Mieder, W. *Tradition and Innovation in Folk Literature*. Hanover and London: University Press of New England, 1987.

Nakhimovsky, A. S. *Laughter in the Void. An Introduction to the Writings of Daniil Kharms and Alexander Vvedenskii*. Vienna: Wiener Slawistischer Almanach, Sonderband 5, 1982.

Perrie, M. "Popular Socio-Utopian Legends in the Time of Troubles" *Slavonic and East European Review* 60, no. 2, 1982.

Piatigorskii, A. "Zametki o 'Metafizicheskoi situatsii'" *Kontinent* 1 (1974): 211-224. Translated as Remarks on the "Metaphysical Situation" in *Kontinent*, 51-62. New York: Anchor Press, 1976.

Prawer, S. *Heine's Jewish Comedy. A Study of his Portraits of Jews and Judaism.* Oxford: Clarendon, 1983.

Quispel, G. *Gnostic Studies.* 2 vols. Istanbul, Leiden: Nederlands Historisch-Archaeologisch Instituut, 1974.

Rabinowitz, S. trans. and ed.. *The Noise of Change: Russian Literature and the Critics 1891-1917.* Ann Arbor: Ardis, 1986.

Revzin, I.I. "Notes on the Semiotic Analysis of Detective Novels, with Examples from the Novels of Agatha Christie" *New Literary History* 9, no. 2 (1978): 385-8.

Rose, M. *Alien Encounters. An Anatomy of Science Fiction.* Cambridge: Havard University Press, 1981.

Sandoz, E. *Political Apocalypse. A Study of Dostoevsky's Grand Inquisitor.* Baton Rouge: Louisiana State University Press, 1971.

Scholes, R., and Rabkin, E. *Science Fiction.* Oxford, New York: Oxford University Press, 1977.

Seifrid, T. "Writing Against Matter: On the Language of Andrei Platonov's *Kotlovan*". *Slavic and East European Journal* 31, no. 3 (Fall 1987): 370-387.

Suvin, D. *Metamorphoses of Science Fiction.* New Haven: Yale University Press, 1979.

Suvin, D. "Criticism of the Strugatsky Brothers' Work." *Canadian-American Slavic Studies* 6, no. 2 (Summer 1972): 286-307.

Strugatsky, A. N. "Ispolnenie zhelanii" (Fulfilment of Desires [an essay]) *Literaturnaia ucheba* 6, 1985.

Strugatsky, B. N. "Ar'ergardnye boi feodalizma" (Rearguard battles of feudalism [a printed speech]). *Literator* 14, no. 9 (Mar. 1990).

Strugatsky, A.N., and Strugatsky, B. N. "Cherez nastoiashchee—v budushchee." *Voprosy Literatury* 8, 1964.

——. "Net, fantastika bogache." *Literaturnaia gazeta* (Dec. 3), 1964.

——. "Davaite dumat' o budushchem." *Literaturnaia gazeta* (Feb. 4), 1970.

——. "Zhizn' ne uvazhat' nel'zia" (Interview). *Daugava*, 1987.

——. "Mezhdu proshlym i budushchim" (Interview). *Literaturnoe Obozrenie* 16, no. 9, 1989.

——. "V zerkalakh budushchego." *Literaturnoe Obozrenie* 6, 1989.

Semenova, S. "Ideia zhizni u Andreia Platonova" *Moskva* 32, 1988.

Teskey, A. *Platonov and Fedorov. The influence of Christian philosophy on a Soviet Writer.* England: Avebury Publishing Company, 1982.

Todorov, T. "The Typology of Detective Fiction." *The Poetics of Prose,* 42-52. Cornell: Cornell University Press, 1977.

Vasiuchenko, I. "Otvergnuvshie voskresen'e." *Znamia* 5 (1989): 216-225.

White, J. *Mythology in the Modern Novel. A Study of Prefigurative Techniques.* Princeton: Princeton University Press, 1971.

Wiles, P. "On Physical Immortality. Materialism and Transcendence." *Survey* 56, 57 (1965): 125-143, 142-161. Includes an anlysis of Fyodorov's beliefs on physical immortality.

Yates, F. *The Art of Memory.* Chicago: University of Chicago Press, 1966.

Young, G. *Fedorov. An Introduction.* Belmont, Mass.: Nordland Publishing, 1979.

Ziolkowski, T. *Fictional Transfigurations of Jesus.* Princeton, New Jersey: Princeton University Press, 1972.

Index

Russian and East European Studies
in Aesthetics and the Philosophy of Culture

This series treats such issues as art as a social phenomenon, categories of aesthetic analysis, social origins of taste, mathematical aspects of aesthetic analysis, and the material basis of cultural change. Contributors include distinguished scholars from Russia and other East European countries. The series editor is:

Willis H. Truitt
Department of Philosophy
University of South Florida
Tampa, FL 33620-5550